Wild in Seattle

Wild in Seattle

Stories at the Crossroads of People and Nature

David B. Williams

MOUNTAINEERS
BOOKS

MOUNTAINEERS BOOKS is dedicated to the exploration, preservation, and enjoyment of outdoor and wilderness areas.

1001 SW Klickitat Way, Suite 201, Seattle, WA 98134
800-553-4453, www.mountaineersbooks.org

Printed in China
28 27 26 25   1 2 3 4 5

Design and layout: Jen Grable
Illustrations by Elizabeth Person
Cover illustration: Elizabeth Person

Library of Congress Cataloging-in-Publication Data Control Number: 2024947529

Mountaineers Books titles may be purchased for corporate, educational, or other promotional sales, and our authors are available for a wide range of events. For information on special discounts or booking an author, contact our customer service at 800-553-4453 or mbooks@mountaineersbooks.org.

 Produced with support from the Port of Seattle Tourism Marketing Support Program

Printed on FSC-certified materials

ISBN (paperback): 978-1-68051-765-1
ISBN (ebook): 978-1-68051-766-8

An independent nonprofit publisher since 1960

To Mom, for your inspiration as
an historian and writer and for your
support and encouragement.
You have always been there for me.

Contents

PART III: FLORA AND HABITAT

Author's Note

The essays in this book originally appeared in my newsletter, *Street Smart Naturalist: Explorations of the Urban Kind*. When I began writing the newsletter in January 2021, I had no idea how it would progress. Not only have I found the writing and research to be fun, interesting, and motivating, but I thoroughly enjoy the interaction I have with readers and subscribers. In the more than one thousand comments I have received, none have been negative, and most have been supportive and encouraging. Thanks to them, and my readers, I have been able to take a sampling of those newsletter articles to create this book.

Please note that throughout the book, I avoid the use of *it* to refer to animals and instead use *he* or *she*, or I phrase my sentences to avoid any pronoun. My main reason for doing so is that *it* objectifies animals, as if they were not sentient, living beings who feel pain and loss. In addition, the use of *it* creates a rift, making nature different from us humans, the only species who merits a pronoun other than *it*. (And, of course, our use of pronouns in reference to people is changing too.) All those others out there, those *its*, must be different and, by implication, lesser than us, which is often the first step to discrimination, and in the case of nature, degradation. I hope that pausing to consider that an animal is far more than an *it* will lead us on a path to deeper, more nuanced, and respectful relationships with the natural world.

Introduction

My parents moved to Seattle when I was five years old, so I had the good fortune to spend my formative years here. Like most kids, I played in my neighborhood, exploring neighbors' backyards and nearby green spaces, one of which we called the Ravine. Wooded with a thicket of understory shrubs, it was an untamed landscape with few trails, or at least, adult trails—the kinds of trails that older people subserviently followed, assuming they led from point A to point B. We kids, of course, didn't need those lame trails; we went where we wanted, following the "real" trails we had created.

More than fifty years later, I am still playing in Seattle. I still like to wander in green spaces, on both the adult and the kids' trails, but I also find inestimable joy in more developed areas along sidewalks and amid buildings. Each location offers an opportunity, a place to seek out the unexpected details, to revel in the overlooked stories, to learn from the past, to practice my innate dorkdom, and to engage my curiosity.

My adult journeys also allow me to fulfill what I consider to be my long-term mission: to become naturalized to Seattle. Since I was not born here and, by definition, am a non-native inhabitant, I feel that one way to naturalize myself is to try to adapt to living here in a sustainable and respectful manner, to learn about the connections that bind together and nourish plants, animals, humans, water, and earth. As Robin Wall Kimmerer writes in her renowned book *Braiding Sweetgrass*, "Being naturalized to place means to live as if this is the land that feeds you, as if these are the streams from which you drink, that build your body and fill your spirit."

Kimmerer's words made me realize that I have been pursuing this idea since I moved back to Seattle in 1998. That pursuit grew out of a job I had in my twenties. After college, I moved to Moab, Utah, and became a park ranger at Arches National Park. Walking the trails and leading campfire talks, I was struck by how interested visitors were in the flora, fauna, and rocks of the park. I began to wonder if they thought about the same things at home. I suspected that if they did make these inquiries, they would discover that the

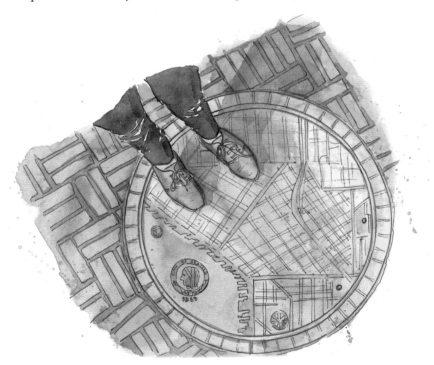

answers were just as interesting, if not more so, than the answers I provided. This led me to encourage people to go home and seek out the natural and cultural history stories around them.

When I returned to Seattle, I actually took my own advice, and over the nearly three decades since coming home, I have continued to pursue these stories. I have been fortunate to share what I have learned by writing several books, including one about stone as a building material, one about Seattle's big land-reshaping projects, and another about Puget Sound. Each weaves together stories of human and natural history, discussions with experts, and observations from my field time.

My goal with the essays in this book is to share some of what I have learned and what has inspired me as I try to naturalize myself. Though most of the essays focus on Seattle, I like to think that they are the type of stories that one could pursue in any urban environment, and ones that will help further your appreciation for the stories found around us in our daily lives. Written as stand-alone essays, they don't need to be read in order, but I think you will benefit from reading them that way.

They begin with geology. Not only are rocks my greatest passion in the natural world, but they also lay the groundwork for understanding the stories of plants, animals, and habitat, as well as have a direct influence on our daily life. For example, in Seattle, it's generally much harder traveling east or west, particularly on foot or by bike, than north or south because of the glacially deposited and carved hills. As I self-avowed geogeek, I think that we in Seattle are fortunate because our geology is so accessible, whether it's our topography, the surrounding mountains we love, or the rock used in downtown buildings. If you haven't considered the world of rocks, I hope these essays inspire you to be impressed by how much geology impacts us, particularly in an urban environment.

RAVINE

Long ago in my less logophilic youth, my friends and I referred to the wooded area close to our homes as the Ravine. Curiously, now that I look back on it, it wasn't really a ravine—which is a narrow, steep-sided valley—and it had an official name: Interlaken Park. Seattle, though, is rife with ravines, most without formal names. We owe this abundance to the last Ice Age and the steep hills, relatively soft sediments, high precipitation, and numerous seeps. *Ravine* is borrowed from the French for "a torrent of water." Other names you might hear elsewhere to describe a similar feature include *gulch*, *arroyo*, *gorge*, *gully*, and *cañada*.

Animals and plants are also central players in the stories of urban nature. Some may be perceived as problematic, such as rats, pigeons, and coyotes; many are overlooked, including horsetails, river otters, and kokanee salmon; and a few are cherished, such as dogs, seals, and Douglas-firs. No matter how we feel about them, all deserve our respect and consideration, having adapted to the challenges of living intimately with people.

The final section is more of a mix, highlighting aspects of the natural world, such as the seasons and habitats, and encounters as diverse as utility poles, the effects of subtle changes in elevation, and historic orchards. I hope these essays can help turn an everyday experience into something new, a reminder to look and pay attention, no matter how well we think we know our neighbors and our community—human and more-than-human.

In addition, as you read the book you will find definitions of words and phrases particular to this place I call home, to the people who inhabit and have inhabited it, who have adapted to it, and who have been informed by living here. Some of the terms that comprise this lexis of place are home grown, others have been adapted and adopted in order to provide clarity or elucidation, and a few are used far beyond our fair city; all are part of the story of this place and, I think, a way to further connect to what makes Seattle Seattle.

Ultimately, I hope to encourage you to get outside and explore your surroundings. I can't help but think that you will be surprised and rewarded by what you discover.

PART I:

Geology

Becoming a Geogeek

Forty years ago I took a class that changed my life and ultimately led me down the path that resulted in this book. I didn't know it at the time, nor had I even thought of taking the class when I went to college. I had originally planned to get some sort of engineering degree, as I hoped to design bicycles. But after getting a 16 percent on a three-hour quiz in physics, and struggling in calculus, I concluded I needed to reconsider my options. Fortunately, I had taken Introduction to Geology prior to the physics classes and realized that I was much better at field trips than engineering principles (in physics, our lone field trip was to the classroom's front door to talk about momentum or inertia or something equally obscure).

I still remember our first geology class field trip. We walked about a half mile from campus to a road cut, basically the geology world's equivalent of seeing a cadaver; it was Anatomy 101 as we got to see under the skin of the earth into the tissues below. Our professor asked us to draw what we saw and label the different rock layers. I don't remember what I drew, but do remember him telling us that we needed to look beyond the colors and to notice the textures and the ways the different layers intersected. It was my first lesson in truly paying attention to the natural world.

I did eventually major in geology and soon moved to Moab, where geology became central to my existence. During my nine years in Moab, I made two discoveries that still resonate with me. I discovered that I liked knowing why the landscape I treasured looked like it did, and I started to expand my narrow geocentric view toward one that still guides me today, looking for connections between plants, animals, rocks, and humanity. I realized that the influence of geology could be seen everywhere, tying together the landscape into a complex quilt of life.

I still frame my worldview through geology, even in Seattle's very urban landscape. When my wife and I moved back to Seattle after I had been gone for fifteen years, I immediately found a connection to the world of rock by studying the geology of the city's building stones. Further explorations led me to learn about the fault zones under the city, how they influenced Seattle's origins, and how our glacial past contributes to drainage issues, where plants grow, and even street names.

Consider, for example, Spring Street, named because of a spring that was once a source of drinking water in early Seattle. The water resulted from the interplay between two layers deposited during the last Ice Age. If you cut open any hill in Seattle, you will find the lower one-third to one-half consists of clay. The next one-third to one-half of the hill is sand and silt, topped with a thin layer of till. When precipitation falls, it percolates through the till and sand until it reaches the impermeable clay and follows gravity and emerges as a seep, or spring, that waters the landscape.

My interest in all things rocky has continued to be essential to helping ground me in the city and to finding the connections to place that are so important to me. I revel in how the region's geologic past influences where I ride my bike, the trails I hike, and the potential disruption (earthquakes, landslides, and volcanoes) that will come to pass. I did not expect to develop this lifelong interest when I took that Introduction to Geology class in college, but I am glad I did. The connection between the deep past and my long-term joy in life is one that I treasure every day.

The Joy of Rock

From a geological point of view, we sort of got ripped off in Seattle. Despite the many ways that geology influences our daily lives, hardly any rock occurs here at the surface. You can find layers of recently deposited sediments at places such as West Point in Seattle's Discovery Park, and you can look out from the city and see great piles of rocks in the Cascades and Olympics, but try to stub your toe on bedrock in Seattle and it won't be easy. So I am always excited when I have an opportunity to put my hands and feet directly on a good old chunk of hard rock within city limits.

Where can you do this, you might wonder? Several areas come to mind. None of them cover much ground, and each is topographically anomalous. Three of the areas form low hills south of downtown, one east and two west of the Duwamish River. A fourth is at Alki Point, on the western edge of West Seattle.

My guess is that the Alki Point anomaly is the most unnoticed, rising just seventy-five feet above the surrounding land. I myself failed to recognize its elevation for many years, but once I did, I realized the upright oddity of the summit; all of Alki is basically a featureless sand flat and is defined geologically as beach deposits, except for this elevated knob. To geologists, it is a lump of twenty-three-million-year-old turbidity current sediments called

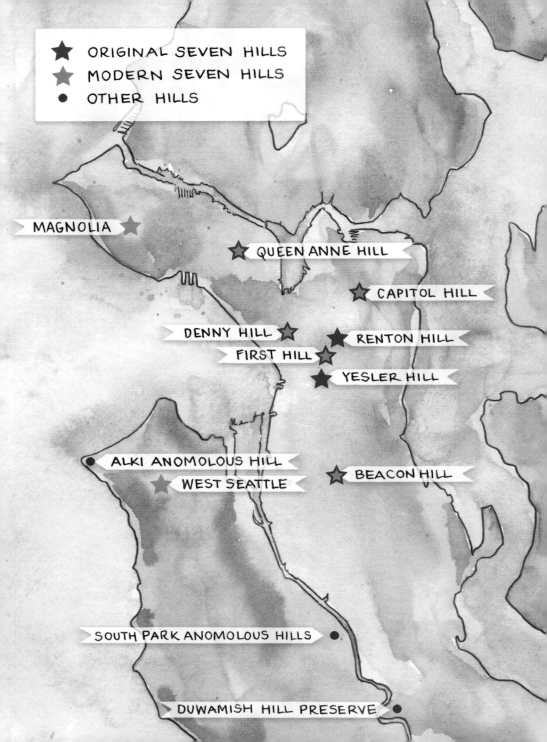

DUWAMISH

The name refers to people of the inside place, or those who lived along what have been named the Duwamish, Cedar, and Black Rivers. As with other words from Lushootseed, the Native language of Puget Sound, the English version approximates the original word, dxʷdəwʔabš. *Absh*, or *ish*, means "people." Today, the Duwamish continue their social, cultural, and economic life through their Longhouse and Cultural Center, near the mouth of the river.

the Blakeley Formation, which most likely used to form a sea stack, possibly connected to land by a tombolo. (Dang, how often does a geogeek get to write *tombolo* and *turbidity* in the same sentence? Clearly not often enough!) At low tide, you can also see the Blakeley as it continues south of Alki Point, part of the reason for good tide pooling in this area.

The Blakeley also forms the two hills west of the Duwamish River in the South Park neighborhood. Unlike the rest of the Duwamish River valley and its relatively flat land, which consists of young (post–Ice Age) horizontal river deposits (which also means this area is highly susceptible to flooding), the hummocks rise to 110 feet. Another idiosyncrasy is that unlike many of the Seattle hills, which tend to be steepest on the east and west sides due to glacial carving, the higher of the two South Park tors drops precipitously on the north. For those parties interested in this abrupt ascent, two stairways (85 and 114 steps) climb the west hill.

The most accessible and tantalizing mound—Duwamish Hill Preserve— rises on the banks of the Duwamish. Protected and planned by a public and private partnership, the preserve has a short trail with steps to the summit and many interpretive signs. I have also read that the knoll provided a vantage point for Native inhabitants to see who was coming and going in the valley. In case you are interested, and I know you are, the rock consists of river-deposited sediments interfingering with volcanic flows and debris. Known as the Tukwila Formation, it formed forty-two to fifty million years ago.

In her 1947 memoir, *When Seattle Was a Village*, early Seattle resident Sophie Frye Bass wrote, "Seattle's hills have been its pride and they have been its problem; they have given the city distinction and they have stood in the way of progress." Sophie was referring to the infamous Seven Hills of Seattle. (Early Seattleites designated these as Beacon, Capitol, Denny, First, Queen Anne, Yesler [also called Profanity], and Renton [or Second], as opposed to modern residents and their seven: Beacon, Capitol, Denny, First, Magnolia, Queen Anne, and West Seattle.) I suspect that she may not have even known of these little geo-anomalies, even though her grandparents Arthur and Mary Denny had landed at Alki Point in November 1851 and became some of the founders of Seattle. Sophie strikes me as an inquisitive sort, so I like to think that she, like me, would extol these hills and their geological delights.

Young and Restless

Few places showcase the dynamic geology of Seattle better than a relatively dull and innocuous-looking riverbank of sediments near downtown. Located close to the mouth of the Duwamish River, the riparian area is part of həʔapus Village Park and Shoreline Habitat, formerly called Terminal 107 Park. (The Westernized spelling of the Lushootseed word həʔapus is *haapoos*, pronounced "ha-ah-poos," and is the name of a small stream draining across a flat on the west side of the Duwamish River.) The site initially drew the attention of researchers in 1975, when workers found mollusk shells during the permit application process for a barge terminal. In several reports published in the 1980s, archaeologists concluded that the area was a midden, or refuse site, where the people who had lived there had tossed the remains of their food, including several types of clams, between the years 670 and 1700.

The reports didn't mention, though, that some of the clams in the nearby riverbank had died abruptly, not due to human activity but to geology. What makes these mollusks noteworthy is that they had lived subtidally but were now well above the tide line. We can blame California for this situation.

Think of Seattle as being trapped in a slow-motion collision. To the south are two train cars: California's Sierra Nevada and Oregon's Coast Range. Plate tectonic movement is shoving the California mountains north into the

Oregon ones, which in turn ram into Washington. But the Evergreen State cannot move because Canada acts as a dead end and resists any northward land migration. As a result, the Seattle area is being squeezed between its two neighbors, creating the Seattle Fault Zone. Running from Issaquah west to Bainbridge Island, the zone is two and a half to four miles wide and has been active for millions of years, slowly thrusting up rocks from the south. In the past ten to fifteen million years, there has been an estimated six miles of vertical movement between the uplifted and down-dropped side of the fault.

Like any good fault, it periodically relieves its stress by cracking. The most recent break occurred 1,100 years ago when an earthquake raised those long dead clams. One minute they were resting quietly in their subtidal homes, and the next they were thrust up twenty-three feet, creating the bank of sediments along the Duwamish River. Topping that bank above the shells is a layer of dark gray sand, which was originally part of Mount Rainier. Coinciding with the movement of mollusks, the mountain erupted and generated a lahar, or a concrete-like slurry of rock, sediment, water, and debris, that poured out of the White River and Duwamish River drainage into Puget Sound, during what is known as the Fryingpan Creek volcanic episode. The lahar was one of several that deposited material into Puget Sound over the past 5,600 years.

The first lahar occurred during a huge eruption of Mount Rainier, when the top one thousand feet or so blew off. At the time, water from Puget Sound extended up what is now the Duwamish valley past Renton and Kent all the way to Auburn. When Rainier lost its head, the resulting lahar, called the Osceola Mudflow, cascaded at speeds in excess of 130 miles per hour down to the Sound, pushing the shoreline north. Each subsequent blast generated another lahar that grew the Duwamish valley and filled in more of the Sound. After the Fryingpan Creek eruption, the lahar sediments pushed the mouth of the Duwamish to its present location. It is these sands that rest atop the invertebrate-choked riverbank, all of which were subsequently uplifted by the Seattle Fault.

For the Indigenous people who lived here at the time, these epic events had a profound effect; many local stories reference a supernatural serpent, known as an *a'yahos*, and specific sites associated with ground shaking. These stories helped provide a way to understand and respect the power of the natural world.

I think modern residents are beginning to understand similar connections between the geologic world and the human world. Seattleites know that our dynamic geology is what makes this such a beautiful place to live,

THE MOUNTAIN

Who knows how long people have been calling the giant peak in the Cascades "the Mountain"? I suspect the nickname for təqʷuʔbəʔ, pronounced "Tahoma" or "Tacoma," the Lushootseed name for Mount Rainier that means "the mother of all waters," dates back forever. The great summit certainly stands out, high above the multitude of lower peaks, and when people first arrived here, the Mountain was about one thousand feet taller. Read the periodic "How Do You Know You're a Seattleite?" columns in the local papers, and you'll see that the use of "the Mountain" always certifies a local, or so say the pundits. Certainly, locals love the Mountain—plus, the term has led to one of Seattle's few weather-specific phrases: "The Mountain is out."

but we are also learning that we inhabit a place with a great potential for catastrophic change. We have been lucky not to have experienced a geological event as significant as those recorded in the bank of the Duwamish, but we would be wise to heed the evidence. If you live in a landscape of young and restless geology, then you need to be prepared for the consequences.

Dead Trees Tell No Lies

Trees die every day of every year, but when the last big Seattle Fault Zone earthquake occurred, something unusual happened: a large number of Douglas-firs perished all at once. These trees have proven to be a critical piece of the puzzle as scientists worked to pinpoint the exact date of that earthquake—one more exact than "about 1,100 years ago."

Relatively shallow, the quake measured about magnitude 7, not much stronger than the 2001 Nisqually earthquake, but with much more significant ground shaking because it occurred closer to the surface. The more details that researchers have about the timing, magnitude, and extent of damage, the better they can model and predict future earthquakes and, they hope, help planners prepare, because when—not if—a similar quake hits again, it will cause billions of dollars in damage and possibly lead to the deaths of numerous people and animals.

In December 1992, geologists published the first evidence of the Seattle Fault Zone. (One of the obvious examples of recent uplift are the anomalous raised beds of rock at Restoration Point, visible from the Bainbridge ferry.) These geologists have long known that the best evidence for a precise date could be found in the annual growth rings of trees, which respond directly to climatic conditions, preserving a detailed record of the history of a tree.

They further knew that the quake created numerous landslides that killed or buried trees across the region. All the geologists had to do was locate the trees, get samples, and read the evidence.

They found what they were looking for in six locations across the Puget Sound region. The farthest south and west is on the Olympic Peninsula at Dry Bed Lake, where rockfalls created a temporary lake that killed trees. About fifteen miles northeast, a quake-induced stream impoundment submerged an entire forest at Price Lake. Researchers sampled twenty-one trees there, including several that required an underwater chainsaw, which sounds sort of nutty and fascinating. Nearby, at Hamma Hamma on Hood Canal, a rockslide dammed a creek, resulting in the formation of another lake that killed another forest, and a few miles west of downtown Seattle, at West Point, the ground snapped and trees died, one of which a tsunami deposited on the beach. This random event may have been witnessed by people who seasonally camped there to harvest shellfish. (Lucky them.) People may also have witnessed an entire grove sliding off the southeast end of Mercer Island into Lake Washington. The trees are still there, standing upright. In 1916, the top of one tree pierced the seventy-eight-foot ferry *Triton* as it carried twenty-five passengers. It sank but no one was hurt. A similar type of landslide also carried trees into the southwest end of Lake Sammamish.

It took the researchers thirty years to collect the trees—which they often did in less-than-ideal conditions—and compare the ring-width patterns. They also compared the trees with an absolute-dated reference set of twenty-seven cores from Vancouver Island that spanned the years 715 to 1990. And, finally, they independently radiocarbon-dated the samples. In September 2023, in a research article in *Science Advances*, an international team reported that they had solved the dating mystery, narrowing the date of the quake(s) to 923 or 924. It is a tour de force and beautiful example of science, taking a unique set of features and combining technology with old-school, out-in-the-field, mucky, muddy detective work to answer an essential question.

What surprised researchers is that there may have been *two* quakes, one on the Seattle Fault and one on the Saddle Mountain Fault (near Lake Cushman, at the south end of Hood Canal), that acted as double blow, rupturing the ground twice within hours to months.

This is not good news. We know that if one quake like this happens, it would be bad. If a second quake struck shortly after, infrastructure and emergency planning, not to forget the landscape itself, would be even more vulnerable to catastrophic issues. But now that these scientists have provided the information on what did happen and what could happen, planners have the opportunity to help build in more resiliency.

All too often in our modern world, people question science and scientists, claiming that they have agendas or are only interested in making money from their research. Over the past twenty-five years, I have interviewed dozens of scientists—in academia, government, and consulting—and have found all of them to be committed to doing the best work they can without any agenda or financial gain. This study exemplifies the core of what scientists do: solve a mystery to help further our understanding of our world, often with the goal of making it a better place.

The Giddiness of Time

As a geogeek who sees the world through obsidian-tinted lenses, I have long been interested in time, particularly what John McPhee called the "deep time" of our planetary past. Stretching back 4.54 billion years, that great abyss of eons is why the world looks as it does. Deep time is what makes possible the ever-so-slow diving of the Juan de Fuca Plate under North America, which gives the Pacific Northwest its dynamic landscape. Deep time is what allowed microscopic organisms to evolve into the myriad of species that grace, have graced, and will grace our little planet. Deep time is what allows me to type this essay using minerals that formed millions of years ago.

Although deep time manifests itself in many ways, it resonates more strongly in some locations. One such place is in downtown Seattle at the southwest corner of Second Avenue and Marion Street. There you will find a rather lovely art deco structure, the Exchange Building, originally built to house the city's commodity exchanges. Alas, it opened in 1930, and the Depression prevented the building from meeting the owners' great expectations. (Talk about bad timing!) But they did choose wisely with their building stone, the Morton Gneiss of Minnesota.

With its swirly pink and black layers, the Morton has a dynamic feel, as if the rock were still forming. In one panel, rafts of jet-black basalt sit like

islands awash in a sea of pink. Other panels look like photographs of blood streaming through arteries, a texture that quarry workers called *veiny*. But the dominant pattern resembles what would happen if you took a series of photos while stirring together cans of pink and black paint—a pattern known as *flurry* in the lingua franca of stone.

More germane to my interests, the Morton Gneiss is 3,524,000,000 years old, or some serious deep time. As naturalist philosopher John Playfair wrote in the eighteenth century, "The mind seemed to grow giddy by looking so far into the abyss of time." The rock is so old that, when it formed, Earth didn't look anything like it does now. The oldest evidence for life is also about 3.5 billion years old, which means that the surface of the planet back then lacked any of the plants or animals or other life-forms that provide the colors and textures and chaos we know today. Instead, the surface's palette was probably fairly muted except for the shades of water and lava. Nor were there any of the sounds that began to come into existence relatively recently.

Furthermore, 3.5 billion years ago is so deep in time that the planet may not have functioned as it does at present. The basic way geology works, as has been taught for fifty years or so, is plate tectonics. The surface of the earth consists of slabs, or plates, in constant motion. Their jostling is responsible for earthquakes, volcanoes, and all the major planetary processes. But one question remains: When did plate tectonics begin? The answer ranges from one billion years ago to three billion or earlier. In other words, the geological processes that formed the Morton Gneiss may or may not have been ones that operate at present, just about one of the most mind-blowing geological concepts I know of.

Whenever I lead building stone tours in downtown Seattle, I always stop by the Exchange Building. I tell people that the Morton Gneiss is most likely the oldest rock they will ever see. It's the oldest one I will ever see, because any older rocks are a long way from anywhere in Canada's Northwest Territories. I also urge them to touch the Morton Gneiss, to reach back, back, back to the early days of Earth and bond with the deep time that binds us all together.

Well-Traveled Cement

After living in Seattle for more than forty years, I uncovered another layer of the geological delights of the urban world: cement used in downtown Seattle buildings originated across the Pacific Ocean more than two hundred million years ago. I discovered this when my wife and I visited San Juan Island.

From the 1860s to the 1930s, San Juan Island was a principal lime supplier to the cement industry in Washington. Production began in 1859 with the British using beds of limestone on the west side of the island and continued through various owners into the early twentieth century. The process is straightforward. Take limestone, which, by definition, is a rock composed of calcium carbonate ($CaCO_3$), or calcite, and burn it at a high temperature, which drives off the carbon dioxide (CO_2) and is the reason why the production and use of cement contributes to global warming. The remaining material, CaO, is known as quicklime.

When quicklime is mixed with water—a process known as slaking—the reaction produces lime putty, or calcium hydroxide [$Ca(OH)_2$]. Lime putty can be used by itself or mixed with an aggregate to make mortar and cement. Because lime putty gets better with age, the Romans, who were premier users of cement, waited at least three years to use theirs.

The kilns the British built on San Juan Island were huge structures made of brick and rock. Using wood, which led to deforesting San Juan and other islands, the workers heated up to fifteen tons of limestone at a time to 1,800 degrees Fahrenheit. Within twenty-four hours, the limestone had become lime. Workers then collected it in barrels weighing 200 to 250 pounds and transported it to warehouses where it remained until shipping.

Several years ago at Stonefest, an annual gathering of rock geeks (carvers, sculptors, and stonewall builders) at the Marenakos Rock Center in Issaquah, I had the good fortune to watch the making of lime. We were taught by Irish stonemason Patrick McAfee, who helped us build a wee kiln to drive away that nasty old CO_2 from the limestone. "We are in a parallel universe for the next four days," said Patrick, as we made use of technology similar to what the Romans would have used, and which was used on a far grander scale in the furnace relics I saw at Lime Kiln and Roche Harbor on San Juan Island.

The cement boom in Seattle began after its Great Fire of 1889, when the city passed ordinances requiring stone and brick as building materials. With these ordinances, lime from the San Juans became more common in Seattle and other cities around Puget Sound for use as mortar or cement, as well as the subsequent use of it in concrete for buildings and structures. Unfortunately, I have not been able to find a list of buildings that used San Juan lime, but Boyd Pratt, who has written the best history of the site and its products, told me that he suspects that "most Seattle masonry buildings, pre-Portland cement . . . would have used San Juan lime."

Part of what makes the local lime intriguing, and adds to my appreciation of urban geology, is the fact that the limestone on the San Juans did not form there. Fossil fusulinids (a type of single-celled organism called Foraminifera) from the Lime Kiln quarries indicate that the limestone formed in the western Pacific Ocean, near Asia, around 248 million years ago.

Because basalt surrounds the Lime Kiln limestone, which occurs in isolated lenses of hardened sediment, geologists propose that the original depositional environment was a seamount atoll ringed by a reef. The basalt erupted into the water via volcanic vents, cooled into pillow-like shapes, then tumbled into deeper water, where it was periodically covered in unconsolidated, calcite-rich, lightly fossiliferous mud, which eventually became the

San Juan limestone. Millions of years later—sometime between eighty-four and one hundred million years ago—plate tectonics carried the basalt and limestone east and accreted, or attached, it to North America.

I can't help but be pleased knowing that the cement used in buildings around Seattle is so well traveled and so old. From Asia across the Pacific Ocean to North America, it minded its own business for tens of millions of years, then traveled from San Juan Island down (or up, as they would have said back in the late 1800s) to Puget Sound, as well as down to San Francisco. So next time you're downtown, take a minute to appreciate the concrete and mortar in the older buildings and the lives entombed within. Their stories began a long, long time ago in an ocean far, far away.

Urban Stalactites

More often than not geology tends toward stasis, with little happening, but if you pay attention, you can be pleasantly rewarded by its subtle manifestations. Riding the light rail to Sea-Tac Airport, I noticed a curious geological feature at the Tukwila station. Hanging down from the platform were stalactites, those classic cave structures. Also known as calthemites (from the Latin *calx*, meaning "lime"; *théma*, meaning "deposit"; and *-ita*, a suffix indicting a rock or mineral), the urban ones in Tukwila were a half inch to several inches long and resembled soda straws. And then, the train left the station, and my little geological moment ended.

The key to calthemite formation is the weathering of concrete and its constituent limey cement. When water penetrates the concrete and seeps along fractures, it can pick up and carry calcium hydroxide. If the water reaches a surface that is in contact with air, the calcium hydroxide mixes with atmospheric carbon dioxide and leads to the formation of urban stalactites made of calcium carbonate, which also happens to be the active ingredient in Tums.

Water in concrete, particularly where calthemites form, comes from precipitation, gutters that leak, air conditioners, sewer pipes, and the like, says Garry K. Smith, an Australian caver and expert on calthemites. He found that stalactite growth depends on drip rate, with maximum growth (0.08

CHINOOK JARGON

The lingua Cascadia of post-settlement Pacific Northwest grew out of vast trade works initially between widespread Indigenous groups and later with European explorers and traders. Most words come from the Chinook language spoken at the mouth of the Columbia, along with elements of Nootkan and Salish dialects and other Native languages, as well as French and English. Chinook Jargon crops up in place-names such as Alki ("by and by" or "in the future"), Tumwater (the waterfall), Tukwila (hazelnut), and Skookumchuck (raging water), as well as in words such as *potlatch* (give) and *muckety-muck* (*muck-a-muck* means "food").

inches per day) occurring when there are eleven minutes between drips. That growth rate is up to 360 times faster than occurs in caves. The longest calthemites are up to a yard long, but most are less than eight inches. Garry told me that if the rate is too fast, on the order of one drip per minute, no stalactite forms, though a stalagmite may develop below the drip.

Calthemites are quite varied in texture and color, though most are white to taupe. The different hues result from metals encountered by the water during its travels through the concrete. Copper pipes lead to shades of green and blue, and steel rebar imparts orangish reds. Halite (table salt) can also affect calthemites but mostly in the surface topography. If left undisturbed, urban stalactites can last indefinitely, says Garry, but they are hollow and could break because of wind or being bumped by a person or beast. He notes that another problem is that the alkaline, or basic, chemistry of the drip can damage car paint, which would probably trigger removal, or at least staunching water movement.

In Seattle, calthemites form in a variety of locations, including tunnels, overpasses, the undersides of bridges, parking garages, and basements. (With all the graffiti covering these types of locations, they're sort of like our own small-scale, modern Chauvet Cave.) The key, as noted above, is concrete, as well as water. As we Seattleites try to deal with what seems to be our new normal of hot summers, what could be better than exploring for urban stalactites in a dark place underground or under a big concrete structure? Have fun.

When Fill Fails

In August 2023, Sound Transit announced that it had to reduce service on its Link light rail because the tracks at Royal Brougham Way, adjacent to the baseball stadium, were sinking and "susceptible to flooding." The stated reason, as reported in the *Seattle Times*, was that the tracks were built on fill that "succumbed over many years." Succumbed to what—gravity, decay, gribbles? (Gribbles are tiny marine isopods blamed for the deterioration of Seattle's seawall.) Let's simply chalk it up to time and its ravages across the urban infrastructure, particularly in the area where the tracks run.

Although we refer to what the kingdomes (as I call the new stadia) are built on as "land," that might not be the best term. The area where Lumen Field now sits once was the tideflats of the Duwamish River. Underwater at high tide and exposed at low tide, the tideflats were an important harvesting area for Indigenous people. When Europeans arrived, however, the protean nature of the tideflats troubled the newcomers because they could not take advantage of what they thought should have been a good location for development.

A solution arrived in 1876 when former chief of police Joe Surber floated a scow to Atkin's Wharf at what is now First Avenue South and South King Street and began to drive logs into the Duwamish mud with a pile driver.

His plan was to pound piles, most likely Douglas-fir trunks up to sixty-five feet long, into the tideflats, which consisted of mud thirty feet deep. After he completed the line of piles across the tideflats, workers built a trestle, which stood several feet above the highest tides, and then laid train tracks atop it for Seattle's second train system, the Seattle and Walla Walla Railroad. (The first trains carried coal between Lake Union and Elliott Bay.)

Trains began to run on March 7, 1877, though they had to compete with couples who liked to promenade on the tracks on Sundays. Within a year, however, voracious burrowing clams called shipworms had destroyed Surber's pilings, and the tracks were unusable. The railroad company's solution? Pound piles for a trestle closer to Beacon Hill, more or less following today's Airport Way.

Once Seattleites realized they could build over the tideflats, they began wholesale altering, pounding in thousands of piles and building trestles and wharves for industry. They also dumped trash and other debris under the infrastructure in order to create fill, or new land. This was not a new process; in the 1850s, Dutch Ned, an employee of Henry Yesler, who built Seattle's first sawmill, had dumped sawdust from Yesler's mill into the area around First Avenue (then known as Front Street, because it was the waterfront) and Yesler Way (formerly Mill Street, for the mill) to raise the land above the high tide line.

By 1920, the tideflats had been completely converted to new land. The most significant fill came from a project envisioned by Washington's former territorial governor Eugene Semple. It began in 1895 and involved moving sediment from one part of the tideflats to another, where it was deposited behind a permeable barrier (made of pilings, brush, and trees) until the new ground surface was two feet above high tide. Other fill came from a failed attempt to cut a canal through Beacon Hill (1901–04), the Jackson Street

regrade (1907–09), and the Dearborn Street regrade (1909–12). Only a tiny amount of sediment from the Denny Hill regrade was used on the tideflats, and none for the creation of Harbor Island, despite what you may read otherwise. Eventually, about 1,300 acres of new "land" replaced the tideflats; none of the builders attempted to tamp down or stabilize the fill, which is why

PRISM LIGHTS

Embedded in the sidewalks of Pioneer Square are small pieces of purple glass, typically square on top with a wedge or prism base below grade. Builders used these prism, or vault, lights to illuminate the underground walkways and storage areas beneath the sidewalks, which were created when the city raised streets after the Great Fire of 1889. Manganese dioxide in the glass, which had long been used to help make glass colorless, creates the color because it turns purple under long-term exposure to ultraviolet light. In 2011, Seattle University professor Marie Wong helped organize a team to study and report on the lights. They counted 27,417 prisms, of which 12,837 were completely intact. Prism lights are found in cities around the world.

during earthquakes it tends toward liquefaction, or what has been likened to becoming Jell-O-like, but no one wants to say that their building or tracks are constructed atop Jell-O.

As one might expect, people soundly criticized Sound Transit for failing to account for the fill and subsidence. Those people seem to think that Sound Transit had no clue about what they were doing, but in reality, the transit authority did extensive geotechnical work and knew that they were building across a landscape made of trash, sand, silt, and other debris. During my research, I was also told that railroads regularly have to fix areas of subsidence, whether on solid land or on fill; that light rail is generally heavier than other passenger trains; and that it would be extremely expensive to build a foundation able to withstand all the expected changes.

If you have walked around Pioneer Square, you have probably experienced subsidence there—tilted sidewalks and parking lots being the most obvious examples. Some buildings have sump pumps to remove water that seeps into their basements, particularly during high tides when water creeps through the seawall and raises the level of groundwater. So, it's not surprising that the light rail tracks are failing. The bigger concern is that Royal Brougham Way is merely the first of more subsidence issues to come for Sound Transit.

Shipping News

I have long been fascinated by ballast, the material carried by ships in order to provide stability. My interest first began when I was researching the use of slate in Boston, particularly for the city's early tombstones. I had read that those tombstones were made of slate that had arrived from Wales in the bottoms of ships. When I tried to find any primary evidence, such as ship ladings or contemporary documents, I couldn't, in part because slate wouldn't have made a great ballast. Ballast typically consisted of ceramic trash, river cobbles, or other small, easily moved rock. (Pliny the Elder, though, wrote of a Roman ship using roughly 240,000 gallons of lentils for ballast.) Taking advantage of the diversity of materials, archaeologists have started to study ballast (sadly, none seem to focus on lentils) as a way to track the travels of ships and have been able to flesh out trade routes across the globe.

With its early maritime-based economy, Seattle relied heavily on ballast, which resulted in one of the city's more infamous landscapes: Ballast Island, near Washington and Second Streets. As the name implies, the island was born out of merchant ships dumping their ballast after arrival in Seattle. At present, ships carry water as a stabilizing ballast, which creates its own problems, such as transporting invasive species. Historically, when ships arrived in port with ballast of rocks and bricks, it was dumped where the ships docked.

Reflecting the international trade, ballast rock from Valparaíso, Sydney, Boston, and Liverpool also ended up here, wrote J. Willis Sayre in *This City of Ours*. Although this list shows up repeatedly in books about Seattle, and there is no reason to doubt Sayre's observation of where the ballast originated, no extant references from that era support it either. Many early articles in the *Daily Intelligencer* asked why the city didn't use the ballast for something useful, such as filling in wharves or macadamizing roads. The stone could be collected and broken up for the roads by "city prisoners . . . at a trifling expense," noted an editorial published on January 29, 1877.

Ballast Island soon grew large enough to show up on maps and in photographs, with the latter typically featuring canoes and tents. Ironically, the artificial island made of exotic rocks was one of the few spots in Seattle where Native people were tolerated, notes Coll Thrush in *Native Seattle: Histories from the Crossing-Over Place*. In addition to being a stopover for Indigenous workers from outside the region who were headed to jobs in the hop fields to the south, Ballast Island became a refuge for locals, including several Native families who had been burned out of their homes in West Seattle by white settlers. By the late 1890s, Ballast Island had been subsumed by the growth of the railroads, and the Native people had been forced from this refuge. It's still there, under pavement, and remains a testimony to Seattle's historic racism. In Thrush's sobering language, Ballast Island exemplified how "urban development and Indian dispossession went hand in hand."

The Ballast Island deposits became newsworthy again in 2014 because of our infamous tunnel-boring machine, Bertha, which had developed a few issues requiring orthodontic reconstruction of its cutting teeth. A year earlier, Bertha had begun to cut a 1.7-mile tunnel for State Route 99 under downtown Seattle, but it had hit a buried steel pipe, which damaged the machine's 57.5-foot-diameter cutting head. During the excavation to reach and repair Bertha, archaeologists unearthed sand, silt, pebbles, brick, and wood, as well as cobbles (about as big as size 3 soccer balls) and boulders of yellowish-brown sandstone. They found no artifacts or other evidence of Native occupation.

One of the archaeologists happened to be in San Francisco soon after the dig. Curious about the stone he had seen in Seattle, he walked over to Telegraph Hill. The sandstone looked exactly like what he had seen in Seattle. He was not surprised. Since San Francisco was the city's earliest trading partner, rock from there was the original and most abundant source for Ballast Island.

SKID ROAD

In historian Murray Morgan's classic tale of the city, *Skid Road: An Informal Portrait of Seattle*, he described Skid Road as "the place of dead dreams." The term *skid road* originated in logging camps in reference to the mud or corduroy roads on which logs would be skidded down to mills. It first appeared in Seattle in the 1850s for Henry Yesler's skid road that brought logs down what was then Mill Street (now Yesler Way) to his waterfront mill. Like the street name, Skid Road changed, becoming Skid Row—and a synonym for less-than-desirable parts of town. Whether the term originated in Seattle or Vancouver, BC, or elsewhere still gets historians hot under their tweed jackets.

Individual ships dumped as much as three hundred tons of rock and sand from quarries on Telegraph Hill into Elliott Bay.

I know of one other connection between San Francisco and ballast. Out on the Washington coast, in the town of Oysterville, are several homes made from lumber often described as "redwood ballast." Back in the 1860s, Oysterville supplied Olympia oysters to San Francisco, whose citizens had an insatiable desire for the Pacific Northwest's most edible native mollusk. Limited amounts of wood and no mill led Oystervillians to seek out good lumber in any way they could, and one source was in the bottom of ships that arrived from California for oysters. A splendid means of acquiring building supplies, *ballast*—which is more often heavy, dense, and doesn't float—is not the best word to describe the light and buoyant redwood. Instead, one might be inclined to refer to said redwood as dunnage, or material used to secure, stabilize, and protect cargo transported in containers.

No matter the source or the material, ballast seems to have achieved a slightly mythical status. I have read of it being used (with good evidence) for paving, buildings, and artwork. In many places, though, it was simply dumped and forgotten, which seems a horrible end for any type of rock, particularly rocks so invaluable to sailors worldwide.

Slip Sliding Away

This process [landsliding] has gone on . . . from a time to
which the memory of man runneth not back.
—Reginald Heber Thomson, City of Seattle engineer, February 27, 1897

It is no small thing to re-engineer the basic geology of the region,
which is what the Plaintiff's position would lead to.
—Kathleen Learned, King County Superior Court judge, July 1999

Our local geology is rarely out of the news cycle in Seattle. On January 7, 2022, *Seattle Times* reporters wrote of a man being rescued from his house on Perkins Lane, in the Magnolia neighborhood, after a rain-saturated slope above the house slid and moved it fifteen to twenty feet off its foundation. Fortunately, no humans were injured, but sadly, one of the family's dogs died.

This was not the first time that stable Perkins Lane structures had been transformed into mobile homes. Twenty-five years prior, the situation was far worse and far more damaging. In late December 1996, several inches of wet snow fell, followed by what we now call an "atmospheric river." When the rains hit on January 1 and 2, they rapidly melted the snow, saturating the ground and triggering landslides that damaged scores of houses, several beyond repair.

The other culprit in these landslides was the last Ice Age and the three layers of sediments the glacier deposited. In addition to creating seeps and springs, the interaction between the lower layers leads to water accumulating atop the impervious clay, which creates a slippery surface susceptible to sliding.

As Mr. Thomson noted above, we have long known of the challenges of Seattle's topography and geology. Attempting to combat the issue, 150 workers began a Works Progress Administration (WPA) project in 1936 to dig drainage trenches into the slopes above Perkins Lane. The plan was to provide conduits to collect water and funnel it away in order to reduce the potential for landslides. It would require "men who are inexperienced, underfed and unwilling, [to work] in trenches 15 to 25 feet in depth where the saturated ground is moving and under unfavorable weather conditions," according to a city council memorandum. Crews eventually dug and lined about 2,500 feet of trenches, with one extending more than 700 feet into the hill and ultimately reaching 100 feet below the surface.

Despite the efforts of the WPA crews, the slopes of Perkins Lane still gush water. And, if you have walked the stairs between Magnolia Boulevard and Perkins, you know the bluff isn't stable, because the stairs make you feel drunk; they are so uneven, tilted, and mismatched. I understand why people choose to live along the road—the quietness and great views—but you couldn't pay me to live there. I once took a geology field trip around Seattle with a bunch of geoengineers who regularly pointed out similar areas with unstable slopes and said the same thing: "I wouldn't live there or there or there." Some builders seem to possess a sense of arrogance, as if they think they can out-engineer nature. As we have long seen, however, at the intersection of the geologic time scale and the human time scale, humans rarely come out on top.

Tsunamis in the Tsound

I am not much of cell phone user, but I do like the periodic ways it keeps me in touch with the world, such as getting a tsunami advisory on my phone. It was triggered on January 15, 2022, by a massive underwater eruption near Tonga, almost six thousand miles from Seattle. The advisory was similar to my first ever tornado advisory for Seattle, which I received two months earlier on November 9. Neither event played out, but I still appreciate the alerts. I suspect that it will not be the last tsunami warning I get.

Geologists, ethnographers, and archaeologists have found evidence for several tsunamis that lashed down Puget Sound and the Strait of Juan de Fuca. The one with the best geological evidence, at least around Seattle, results from the last movement of the Seattle Fault Zone in 923 or 924. The crustal zone of weakness created a tsunami when its south side thrust up and caused a displacement of water that led to waves spreading across the Sound, one of which deposited the trunk of a Douglas-fir (researchers used this tree's tree rings to help date the earthquake) and a fine layer of sand on the beach at West Point in Discovery Park. (A similar displacement of water also occurred in the Tonga eruption, which led to the tsunami advisory.)

Other tsunami deposits include one at Lynch Cove, near Belfair at the tip of Hood Canal. In geologist Carrie Garrison-Laney's PhD dissertation, she describes two layers of silt at Lynch Cove deposited by a tsunami generated by earthquakes off the Washington coast. The most recent of these earthquakes occurred on January 26, 1700, when what is known as the Cascadia Subduction Zone ruptured. This means that tsunamis can make a ninety-degree turn at Admiralty Inlet and then turn again to enter Hood Canal. As my wife would say, physics did that.

Although the evidence is not clear, recent work by archaeologists suggests that when past tsunamis hit, they affected the people living in the region. At Discovery Bay, at the east end of the Strait of Juan de Fuca, it appears that one tsunami caused the temporary abandonment of a village. Movement of the Seattle Fault and the subsequent tsunami also caused abandonment of several villages around the Sound and may have led to the change of one site from a summer fishing and clamming camp to a major winter village.

For thousands of years, the active geologic nature of this place has permeated the collective psyche of the region, shaping how and where we live. My hunch is that modern residents are proud of and exhilarated by the geology, but they are also nervous about it. (Residents of earlier eras, particularly

TORNADO   TSUNAMI   VOLCANO

JUAN DE FUCA

In 1596, Greek mariner Apostolos Valerianos told English merchant Michael Lok that he had sailed north from Mexico to a "broad Inlet of Sea" between 47 and 48 degrees latitude. Valerianos, who is better known as Juan de Fuca, sailed east for more than twenty days, finding a productive land and valuable minerals. He thought he had discovered the Straits of Anian, or the legendary Northwest Passage. He didn't, and his name remains, though most historians doubt that Juan de Fuca ever made it to his eponymous strait.

geologically dramatic ones, learned to adapt.) I don't think residents would want it any other way—we recognize that our geology is what makes this such a beautiful place to live, even with all the potential damage that can ensue.

The other outstanding feature of the 2022 Tongan eruption (which generated about a foot-high wave in the Sound) is that the volcano produced an atmospheric ripple that traveled the globe at 820 miles per hour and temporarily blew away the fog in Seattle. I just have to proclaim, "Golly Ned. That is totally amazing." As they say, it's a small, round planet we inhabit.

Return to the Ice Age

My wife and I recently returned to the Ice Age, or what geologists call the Last Glacial Maximum (LGM). Sadly, we were not in a time machine, because if I could go back to any point in time, I'd head straight to some prominent knoll to watch the great Missoula floods. Superagents of erosion during the LGM (now you can see why I introduced the abbreviation because it saves me from having to write out *last Ice Age*), those floods were some of the most amazing geological events of the past 4.5 billion years.

The floods began at Glacial Lake Missoula in western Montana, which had the volume of about six hundred Lake Washingtons, and occurred between twenty thousand and about fourteen thousand years ago. Formed by a massive ice dam, the lake periodically burst through the ice and sent 706 million cubic feet per second of water, or about 2,700 times more than the average volume at the mouth of the Columbia, raging and rippling across what is now northern Idaho, eastern Washington, and the Columbia River Gorge. The onslaught of water, which occurred in at least one hundred separate floods, sculpted the landscape, creating the planet's largest ripples, massive waterfalls, and what surely must have been ginormous towheads, or sandbars and shoals. (I admit I dropped *towhead* in because I just learned

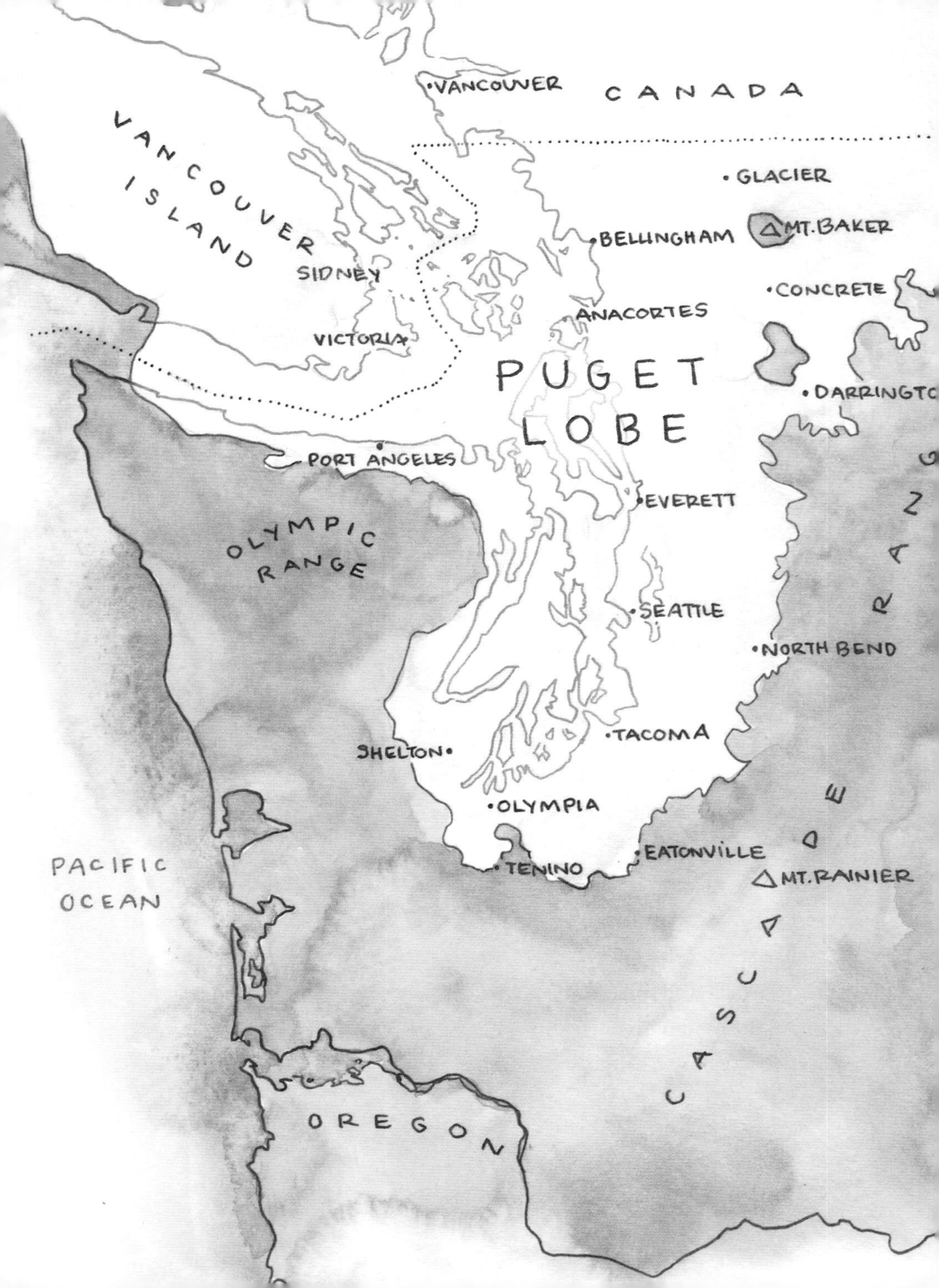

VANCOUVER
CANADA
VANCOUVER ISLAND
GLACIER
MT. BAKER
BELLINGHAM
SIDNEY
CONCRETE
ANACORTES
VICTORIA
PUGET LOBE
DARRINGTO
PORT ANGELES
EVERETT
OLYMPIC RANGE
SEATTLE
NORTH BEND
TACOMA
SHELTON
OLYMPIA
EATONVILLE
TENINO
PACIFIC OCEAN
MT. RAINIER
CASCADE RANGE
OREGON

what it meant.) Now you know why I'd want to see these epic floods . . . and be up on a high ridge away from the water.

I know that I will never see a geological event as astounding as these floods, but sometimes the right climatic conditions allow me the joy of pretending the possibility exists. Such was the case when we were hiking the Oyster Dome Trail, up above Chuckanut Drive just south of Bellingham, and we emerged out of the trees at the top and found ourselves in glorious sunlight. Below us, a fog sea covered the Salish Sea. To the southwest rose the Olympic Mountains, and slightly north was the top of Lummi Island. It wasn't exactly what the Puget lowland would have looked like during the LGM, but it gave a good feel: a massive stretch of white that extended south to about Olympia, with high foothills and the Cascade and Olympic Mountains poking above and covered in much larger alpine glaciers than at present.

One significant difference is that the Oyster Dome (2,025 feet) would have been covered by ice. Based on glacially abraded bedrock and glacial erratics (more on these in the next essay), geologists have determined that the glacier was three thousand feet thick in Seattle and five thousand feet thick in Bellingham at the ice's greatest extent. In other words, a couple thousand feet of ice would have been above the location where my wife and I were standing, which means, of course, that the sea of ice would have covered a lot more land and ruined our hike.

But still, I like to imagine that what we saw was a tantalizing vision of what happened here many times. Geologists have found evidence for at least seven ice ages in the Puget lowland over the past two million years. Each time the ice plowed south (advancing about a soccer pitch a year), it pushed between the mountain ranges, scraped and shaped, and left behind a tabula rasa eventually pioneered by new ecosystems.

DRUMLIN

To a geologist, the hills of Seattle are drumlins. In the words of early nineteenth-century Irish geologist James Bryce (who lived when and where the term originated), "This peculiar form is so striking that the peasantry have appropriated an expressive name to such ridges . . . the name Drum and Drumlin." Ours formed as the massive Puget lobe of the Cordilleran Ice Sheet moved south and sculpted and compressed the underlying sand, silt, and clay into a series of parallel ridges and valleys, or what we call hills. Note how they tend to be steeper on the east and west sides, as if the ice was slicing open the landscape.

After the ice retreated, or melted, the last time—about 15,500 years ago, at about twice the speed it advanced—the first plants created an open hemlock- and oak-dominated savannah habitat teeming with mastodons, Columbian mammoths, giant sloths, bison (about two times bigger than modern ones), and short-faced bears. They didn't survive long, either due to climate change or too many people hunting the charismatic megafauna, and, sadly, were extinct by about eleven thousand years ago. Continued warming later led to more conifers and denser forests until, by about five thousand years ago, the ecosystem looked like our modern one: a temperate rainforest interspersed with prairies, bogs, and burnt patches, both natural and human enhanced.

How strange would it be if a massive sheet of ice covered this region now, and we could see it only as visitors who had traveled north to experience a world so different from our homes in the ice-free south? We take for granted that we live in an interglacial period, but many generations of our species worldwide inhabited an icy world much more daunting than our present. One advantage, though we seem to be doing our best to counter it, of living in this interglacial time is the relatively benign climate. Even if we compare our modern climate to areas south of the continental ice sheets, which were more hospitable to plants and animals than areas to the north, the conditions today are generally favorable compared to climates on our continent tens of thousands of years ago.

None of us alive today will experience a shift in climate as dramatic as the difference between what exists now and what existed during the last Ice Age. Fortunately, though, the weather occasionally conspires and allows us to time travel and catch a glimpse of that former world.

Erratic Behavior

When I moved east to Boston many years ago, Plymouth Rock was about the sum total of my knowledge of New England geology. Basically, I knew nothing but a name. As it turns out, the Pilgrims' infamous landing point was one of my favorite geologic features, a glacial erratic. If you are not familiar with this flotsam of the Ice Age, you are missing out. Erratics are rocks—technically any size but often noticed because they can be as big as the proverbial school bus—carried by glaciers and then left behind when the ice melts and disappears. After the ice retreated, Plymouth Rock was in the perfect position to provide a stepping stone for the new arrivals, assuming you buy that story of the *Mayflower* migrants, which many do not.

Although New England geology is relatively dull compared to Seattle's active tectonics, it shares a common feature with my fair city. Erratics—a dozen plus—dot the Seattle landscape.

The most famous is the Wedgwood Erratic, also known as the Wedgwood Rock, Lone Rock, or Big Rock (located at the intersection of Northeast 72nd Street and 28th Avenue Northeast). According to local historian Valarie Bunn, it was famous as early as July 4, 1881, when sixteen-year-old Martin Weedin scrambled to the top of the nineteen-foot-tall rock and

ERRATIC

A term first used in the 1820s in Switzerland, *erratic* refers to curious boulders found far from what appeared to be their point of origin. The arrival of the boulders was eventually traced to glaciers that had carried the rocks and deposited them when the ice melted. *Erratic* comes from the Latin *errāticus*, meaning "to wander," certainly an apt description for these peripatetic, glacier-riding rocks.

"read the Declaration of Independence in a very creditable manner," as reported in the *Seattle Post-Intelligencer* on July 6, 1881. The Big Rock continued to attract peak baggers and eventually became a mecca for The Mountaineers, which used it as a classroom. Geologists have determined that the rock rode the ice highway from Fidalgo Island near Anacortes, about seventy-five miles north.

Another outstanding erratic, which is out standing in a field, is one "recently" discovered (in the early 2000s) in Leschi Park, on the western shore of Lake Washington. It was found by people who were clearing the vegetation around it. What makes this one special is that it is chock-full of fossils, in particular, clams in the genus *Buchia*. Since its unveiling, geologists have debated whether the rock came from around Mount Baker or southern British Columbia. They tend to agree that the clams lived about 150 million years ago and are from what is known as the Nooksack Group of rocks.

Intriguingly, those clams have traveled before; the Nooksack Group is part of an accreted terrane, or rocks sutured onto North America by plate tectonic movement. What geologists can't agree on is where the Nooksack rocks originated. Did the tectonic highway carry them from Baja California or someplace else to the west? Either way, the erratic's travels are minimal in comparison to the travels of its parent material.

Not everyone cottoned on to our erratics. At least two, long known and seemingly valued as landmarks, no longer exist: one was at 48th Avenue

South and South Ferdinand Street, and the other at Broadway and Madison Street. Both were locally called Big Rock (seems to me that people could have been more creative with their names, such as the Madison Marvel, the Whopping Boulder of Ginormity, or Ferdinand's Glory Stone) and served as meeting places, and apparently, a bit more. In an October 26, 1892, article in the *Seattle Post-Intelligencer*, an unnamed reporter wrote that the Big Rock on Madison was scheduled to be blown up, noting that in the past "when habitations in that part of the city were few and scattered lovers made it their trysting place . . . fortunately for the lovers who have whispered their confidence under its shadow, the big rock tells no tales." I haven't been able to figure out when Ferdinand's Glory Stone was destroyed.

One person who would have been appalled at Seattleites' boorish behavior regarding erratics was Johann Wolfgang von Goethe. Considered by many to be Germany's greatest writer and philosopher, Goethe was a passionate geogeek, particularly regarding what he called *Granitgeschiebe*, or granite that is shoved. His interest in *die Wanderung der Granitblöcke* (the wandering of granite blocks) began in the 1780s, when he encountered them in Germany, and blossomed in the 1820s, when he wrote about them in *Wilhelm Meister's Years of Wandering*.

Goethe initially thought that giant floating rafts of ice had carried the erratics, or foundlings (*Fündling*), as some called them, but later concluded that sheets of ice were the primary mover. Based on this idea of an icy conveyor belt, Goethe proposed an even more radical notion, that Europe had experienced an "epoch of great cold," or what was soon called the Ice Age. Naturalist Louis Agassiz, who had emigrated to the United States from Switzerland in 1846, is generally credited with popularizing the idea of the Ice Age, but he acknowledged that Goethe "alone unified all the indications into a definite theory."

Goethe is famous for his many life maxims. One of my favorites is "In nature we never see anything isolated, but everything in connection with something else which is before it, beside it, under it, and over it." Sounds to me like he is describing erratics. Rock on, Johann!

Agents of Erosion

My college housemate and I, both geology majors, liked to call ourselves "Agents of Erosion." We didn't do anything to merit the sobriquet; we just thought it was funny, especially if we said it in a supervillain kind of way. "*AAAA-gents of EEE-ROWW-shunnnnn, shun, shun.*" (Geology doesn't have that many funny things about it, so we took what we could.) I am not sure anyone would have agreed with us regarding our status, or our sense of humor, but I am used to that. To be frank, saying Agents of Erosion, even without trying to sound stupendous, still tickles me.

Erosional operatives, such as roots, salt, ice, and acid rain, are everywhere in the urban environment. Some people might more correctly refer to them as "weathering agents," as they merely weaken substrate such as concrete and asphalt and don't ferret away the broken-up bits, the mission of agents of erosion. Both forces are at work in Seattle, and every other town and city.

Winter is the season of reckoning with these nefarious urban forces of dilapidation and disintegration. When it snows, the city puts chains on bus tires, which is necessary for safety but also foments the weakening and cracking of pavement. Cold weather also leads to the growth of potholes. Water has a rather unusual property of expanding when it freezes. (Only a handful of substances do. When most liquids freeze, their molecules slow down, their bonds tighten, and they become more compact.)

The expansion of water translates to potholes, as water infiltrates pavement and turns to ice and cracks its surroundings. This may trouble vehicle drivers in the city, but we need to get over ourselves because that ice expansion (about 9 percent) is a good thing for Earth. If water didn't expand and float when it becomes ice, I wouldn't be here to write this, and you wouldn't be here to benefit from my scintillating prose because lakes would freeze from the bottom up, which would probably benefit no one, particularly anything wanting to live in a lake that could become a solid block of ice. So the next time you hit a pothole, rejoice at the life-affirming origin of the water and ice that formed it.

Less tied to life on Earth but also problematic in the urban environment is salt, another unraveler of the urban fabric. It is particularly troublesome in cities that salt their roads in winter, though salt also arrives from

the atmosphere and wave action. After it has infiltrated concrete or stone, salt crystals begin to grow and weaken the surrounding material. I have to admit that I have taken advantage of how stone cannot withstand salt and ice weathering and have flaked off layers of sandstone building blocks, illustrating that I actually am an Agent of Erosion.

I also have another, more subtle effect in my ongoing role as an Agent of Erosion. And, not to forget all who read this, you, too, play the same role. All of us erode stone stairways, one microbit at a time, as our shoes strike and scrape the granite, limestone, sandstone, or travertine used for stairs. One place to see this in Seattle is Suzzallo Library on the University of Washington campus, where decades of feet have created a slight indent in the travertine tread. The effect is far more pronounced in much older buildings, such as the Leaning Tower of Pisa, Westminster Abbey, and Angkor Wat.

Humans are not the only living agents of erosion. Trees are notorious for the problems they cause with streets and sidewalks, which are no match for the forces roots impart. Ever expanding and spreading, roots buckle, deform, warp, disfigure, contort, and destroy the urban infrastructure. (Gotta love that thesaurus!) On some streets, I feel that I am on the surface of the sea as tree after tree thrusts up the sidewalk, creating regular waves of concrete that make walking difficult. The challenges raised by roots can be costly to cities. From 2020 to 2023, people filed 151 claims related to sidewalk falls against the City of Seattle, which led to the city spending $358,100 in settlements. Because of this issue, the city restricts what trees can be grown along sidewalks, banning bigleaf maple, cottonwood, and willows.

I still like to consider myself an Agent of Erosion, though I know that I pale in comparison to the great agents affecting the urban environment. In contrast to me and my limited time spent wreaking havoc, they are always at work. As they say, nature bats last, as well as first, second, and so on.

PART II:

Fauna

Urban Umwelt in Awe of Animals

From 1994 to 2007, I was part of a small pack consisting of my wife; our dog, Taylor; and me. Beautiful, smart, and enchanting, Taylor was a beloved pal. Of course, I spoiled her, especially in the walk realm, taking her out three times a day throughout her life. (The devoted walker that I am needed little excuse to get out.) As we walked, I noticed that Taylor stopped regularly to take stock of her world. I likened this to reading a letter (she was a pre-texting pooch) and checking in on her community.

Most of the time, I had no clue what drew her attention, but on those rare snowy days in Seattle, I was treated, slightly, to her world. Most obvious was the yellow snow, which revealed the peelegraph (or peemail for more modern folk) network that dogs use to let others know their whereabouts, as well as other personal information far too subtle for me ever to perceive. I could also see the tracks of other animals—mostly dogs, but also squirrels and birds—that she had sensed. It was a true treat to be given a small glimpse into the world of animals that was usually invisible to me.

And it is an astounding world, rich in senses that not only operate in ways ours cannot but also function in ways we cannot imagine. Consider Taylor's nose. When she inhaled, like us, most of the air she breathed in entered her lungs, but some also traveled to the back of her snout and entered a complex maze of thin, bony walls covered in an olfactory layer of neuron-dense tissue. We also possess these olfactory detectors but at levels much less perceptive than Taylor's. In addition, those little slits on the side of her nose altered the flow of her exhalations such that odors circled back into her nose. I can only wonder how this double whammy of olfactory information affects the canine peelegraph network.

A dog's ability to process information by sniffing is just the tip of the sensory iceberg when it comes to animals. Most of us are familiar with

echolocating bats and whales and perhaps magnetoreception in our local salmon, but those oh-so-common, oh-so-overlooked robins in our front yards also possess an internal magnetic compass that aides in migration. Other sensory superpowers include electrolocation, the ability of many species of fish to sense their world via electric currents they produce; UV vision and the ability to see colors the human eye cannot detect that could aid in pollinating and mate selection; and the ability to hear low frequencies, which allows whales to communicate across thousands of miles of ocean.

Despite discovering the many ways animals sense, however, we have no clue what they do with this information. Just because whales can share stories across the ocean, does that mean they do so? How does a starling's faculty to see UV light impact how they interact with their own kind or with other species? What did Taylor do with her awareness that the pooch up the street walked by hours ago? We will probably never know the answers, but by paying attention to the senses of other species, we continue to develop a fuller understanding of our amazing planet, and that can only help us have better regard for animals.

One's sensory perception of the world is known as *umwelt*, a term coined in the early 1900s by Baltic German biologist Jakob von Uexküll from the German for "environment" or "phenomenal world." Each of us, and each species, has a specific umwelt, directly related to our perception and needs. Ed Yong, author of *An Immense World*, which explores the hidden senses of animals, writes that Uexküll's concept of umwelt was a radically different way of viewing and relating to animals. For much of history, people had disregarded the feelings and senses of animals, often seeing them as automatons. Seventeenth-century philosopher Nicolas Malebranche wrote that "animals eat without pleasure, cry without pain, grow without knowing: they desire nothing, fear nothing, know nothing."

What is clear and amazing and extraordinary is that an animal's umwelt is anything but nothing. They see, hear, smell, taste, and touch (as well as navigate) the world around them in so many creative and diverse ways that I cannot help being astonished and humbled. My sensory means, which mostly work fine (aided by reading glasses) and allow me not to make too many boneheaded errors regarding what I sense, are only one way of interacting with the world. How could I ever think my way is better than any other? Clearly, these animals have been and are successful—and many for far, far longer than our relatively new species—in their adaptations to living.

Yong's book is well written, mind expanding, and packed so densely with information that I think the footnotes even have footnotes (toenotes?). Reading it has forever changed my view of the world and how I sense my surroundings. (I originally wrote *see* instead of *sense* but realized that *see* led me to a narrower approach than I now hope to experience my umwelt.) I know that living in an urban landscape limits my encounters with many animals, who, understandably, do not choose to live among us and our often less-than-friendly-toward-animals lifestyles. So, for those who do choose to live among us, and give me the opportunity to be exhilarated with profound awe at the myriad ways that life manifests itself, I am grateful.

Coyotes in Seattle

Walking to the light rail station at Northgate, I heard a wonderful sound. Fifty feet up ahead, I saw the source: a lone coyote standing atop a high spot at North Seattle College. He or she was clearly agitated by a pair of dogs and their people on the grass below. As I stood there watching, the coyote continued to bark, or yip, as well as howl. It was a glorious way to begin my day.

This was not the first time I have seen coyotes around Seattle. I have seen them under I-5 on Northeast Ravenna Boulevard, several times at North Seattle College, and once, I encountered three of them sitting in the middle of an intersection on a quiet road. They didn't seem to care that I was running by them. I wondered if they would have moved when a car arrived; they certainly seemed to own the road.

I am always pleased when I see an urban coyote, knowing that they, both the individual and the species, are survivors who have adapted to the world's number one predator: humans. The US government, via a variety of agencies, has killed millions of coyotes, prompted by concerns that they are vicious predators who, if left uncontrolled, will wreak havoc on an epic scale. A study of media accounts discussing urban coyotes in Canada noted that coyotes were regularly portrayed as brazen, violent, menacing attackers who terrorized, ravaged, and feasted on urban pets. As recently as 2021, the federal

COYOTE

According to Dan Flores's *Coyote America*, the term *coyote*, or *collote*, first appeared in Albert Pikes's *Journeys in the Prairie, 1831–1832*. Pike used the Spanish double *ll*, pronounced as *y*. Before then, many people in the United States called them prairie wolves. The term *coyote* derives from *coyotl*, which is from Nahuatl, an Aztecan language. Nineteenth-century Spanish speakers pronounced coyote as *coy-YOH-tay*, accenting the second syllable. You may also hear *KY-yote*.

government's Animal and Plant Health Inspection Service intentionally killed an average of 7.3 coyotes every single hour of the year.

And yet, coyotes have survived and even thrived. Ironically, one way coyotes have responded to humanity's war on them is by increasing the number of pups they have, which means more survive to head out and move into new territory. Another reason for the spread of coyotes is that they are great teachers, with parents instructing their young on where, when, and how to find food; adults also pass on a wariness and cleverness developed through generations of being persecuted. In addition, they are monogamous and mate for life.

Coyotes are curious, which can be problematic when they are probing the edges of their territory and come into contact with our territories, or what we like to call our yards. Robert Long, senior conservation scientist at the Woodland Park Zoo, explained to me that this has led to a myth that coyotes lure urban pets into the woods, where a pack is waiting to attack. Such an idea is completely unfounded, says Robert, and is more a reflection of our perceptions and how humans tend to project human traits onto animals.

When a pet appears, the coyote will most often retreat to get away from a perceived threat. Unfortunately, the dog may pursue the coyote, which may end up poorly for the dog if he or she runs into the coyote's protective family.

Coyotes are relatively small (about twenty to thirty pounds), do not kill people (dogs kill thirty-five people per year), do not hunt in packs, and are rarely aggressive. More often, and not surprisingly, we create the problems by leaving out food, feeding the coyotes, overreacting, and letting our pets off leash.

We do not know how many coyotes live in Seattle, but given the number of sightings, it seems that quite a few share our cityscape with us. In August 2019, the Woodland Park Zoo started its online Carnivore Spotter program, where you can send in your reports of urban carnivore sightings. More than 4,200 reports were submitted in the first year. About 50 percent were coyotes. Others, in order of number of reports, were raccoon, bobcat, black bear, river otter, opossum, mountain lion, and red fox. Coyotes were seen throughout the day (which is normal) and across the city, with the highest numbers north of the Lake Washington Ship Canal. Like people, coyotes eat pretty much anything, favoring rodents and rabbits, fruit (apples and cherries), insects, and the occasional domestic pet.

Coyotes reaffirm for me a central truth that humans, even ones living in dense urban settings, cannot separate ourselves from the natural world around us. Whether it's weather, migrating geese, morning birdsong, tides, or encounters with mundane species, such as rats, pigeons, gulls, and cockroaches, wildness permeates our urban spaces and plays a role in our daily existence. This not only brings me hope that we will never banish nature but also makes my life more enjoyable, and for that I rejoice. Yay, coyotes!

Of Eagles and Terra-Cotta

Downtown Seattle is a good place to go birding. I have seen pelicans, ravens, and ducks, including several sets of tracks. None are living or produced by an animal; all are adornments on buildings, except the tracks, which some whimsical builder embedded in the sidewalk. I have also counted more than 120 eagles (and close to 300 lions, the most abundant architectural animal). The most formidable eagles are several scowling atop the Camlin Hotel at 1619 Ninth Avenue. I have also seen two that carried the sun, many that are abstract, one that looks guilty, and several seemingly ready to soar. Whenever I am in doubt as to the bird species being depicted, if the image includes a beak and talons, I assume it's an eagle, as these features seem, to me, to be the essence of eagleness.

Nearly all of the urban eagles are molded terra-cotta, a building material that was widely used in the city between the 1890s and 1930s. The reasons were severalfold. It was cheaper and lighter than stone, easier to fashion into any desired shape, and fireproof. Plus, clay, its main ingredient, was easy to obtain, primarily by quarrying the city's hillsides of beds deposited during the previous Ice Age. These clay layers, as well as forty-million-year-old clay deposits found east of Lake Washington, are also why so many buildings and roads in King County were built with brick.

The most aquiferous building was built in 1925 for the Fraternal Order of Eagles as their Aerie No. 1. (The organization started in Seattle in 1898 as the "Seattle Order of Good Things.") The building at 700 Union Street features thirty-three eagles, including a full-bodied, three-dimensional eagle made out of terra-cotta, cast at a cost of $2,100 (around $36,500 today) and described in a City of Seattle landmarks report as "an unprecedented achievement at the time." In addition, an eagle with spread wings sits atop a flagpole on the roof; I once saw a gull sitting on the ersatz eagle.

TERRA-COTTA

Basically a glazed brick, terra-cotta (literally "fired earth") was a popular building material in Seattle. Fabricators create terra-cotta pieces by making a clay sculpture and then a mold of it in plaster. After removing the sculpting clay, workers press malleable clay into the mold, remove the plaster, and glaze and fire the piece. Because of the glaze, the surface color and texture can vary, though Seattle builders primarily used white or a granite look-alike. Seattle has some of the better and more abundant terra-cotta-clad buildings in the country because the preservation movement got started here before the buildings were lost to development.

Dignified, elegant, majestic, and powerful, eagles represent attributes that many people strive toward. I think this is why they appear regularly on buildings; the owners saw the eagles as an advertisement, a shorthand way to convey a simple message: "We who work in this building possess the traits you admire in our national symbol." Or so they hoped we'd think.

We in Seattle and the surrounding region can also experience live Bald Eagles. During the annual Christmas Bird Count, birders regularly find more than fifty balds within the fifteen-mile-diameter count circle centered in downtown Seattle. Bald Eagles may be impressively resilient, but they also needed us to acknowledge our impacts. The rise in their population corresponded directly with the ban on DDT, rules to protect them, and restrictions on harmful industrial practices, such as pulp mills. With respect and honor, we can live together.

I remember my first Bald Eagle sighting in Seattle. My wife and I were walking around Green Lake in north-central Seattle, about a mile from our house, the morning of our first Thanksgiving living here, when one flew over the water carrying a stick. The beautiful bird seemed a good omen for our choice to return to my hometown. I subsequently located the nest and regularly stopped by as a pair of eagles gave birth, hunted in the lake, brought fish back to the nest, and successfully launched their youngster. I also watched as one fish flopped out and fell eighty feet to the ground where crows instantly found it. I have continued to be blessed by their presence; the Green Lake eagles have found the tall Douglas-firs surrounding our house and periodically hang out in them.

Whether hunting over the water, being harassed by crows, or gazing out from a perch, the Bald Eagles of Seattle are a wild gift in the urban world. And if I can't see those wild apparitions, then at least I can head downtown and enjoy their terra-cotta cousins.

Of Seals, Sea Lions, and the Locks

The other day at the Hiram M. Chittenden Locks, I had a new experience. I saw a harbor seal swimming on the freshwater side of the overflow dam. Normally, I see seals and sea lions within the lock gates, where I assume they venture in search of salmon, who often pass from freshwater to saltwater via the locks, but this was the first time I had seen one dallying on the Salmon Bay side. I couldn't tell what the animal was doing—I saw the head only once—but I suspected food was the main attractant.

As I watched, I realized that I hadn't given seals, or their oft-mistaken-for cousins, California sea lions, much consideration. I had seen them many times over the years throughout Puget Sound and along the Pacific coast but hadn't thought about the other places I had seen them, such as in coastal rivers and estuaries. I knew that they were both marine mammals, and thus animals primarily of the sea. I also knew they had evolved to make use of fresh water for short periods of time, but seeing them in a lake seemed odd.

No matter the where, when, and why, it's an amazing adaptation to be able to navigate and inhabit two such different environments; both media

SHIP CANAL

The Montlake Cut and the Fremont Cut make up what is known as the Lake Washington Ship Canal. Chinese workers employed by the Wa Chong Company completed the first cuts linking Lake Washington and Lake Union and Puget Sound in 1885. In 1901, the cut between Lake Union and Salmon Bay was expanded into what was known as the Government Canal. Workers completed the modern Ship Canal in 1916; it opened officially on July 4, 1917, sixty-three years to the day after early settler Thomas Mercer proposed the idea of connecting salt water and fresh water.

may be liquid, but clearly both are not suited to all. As Mr. Coleridge wrote, "Water, water everywhere, nor any drop to drink."

From what I learned from employees at the locks, the seals and sea lions (mostly males) regularly move between Puget Sound and Salmon Bay. They do so in two ways. The simplest, most direct method is by entering the locks when they are open to salt water, waiting until the locks fill with fresh water, and then exiting into the bay. But they don't need to wait; they can also travel via the feeder culverts that run along the sides of the locks and provide the fresh water needed to raise boats, and pinnipeds, from salt to fresh water. No matter how they figure it out—smell, follow the leader, or by accident—it's another fine adaptation to place.

Despite their adaptions to humanity and our inventions, the pinnipeds sometimes get swept away by what we do. A lock employee told me that she recently saw a group of young sea lions on the freshwater side near the overflow dam, when one of them, who seemed to be trying to figure out how to return to the salt, got carried by the current through the smolt gate, which shoots water from the bay to the Sound. "I heard a little bloop sound and down he went.... When I turned to see the sea lion below, his head was snapped around looking back toward the slide like, 'What just happened?'"

This passage through the Ballard Locks is not the first time that harbor seals have adapted to fresh water in the region. During the last Ice Age, as the Puget lobe glacier melted back to the north, freshwater lakes—glacial Lake Bretz and Lake Russell—formed and covered much of the Puget lowland. They existed for several hundred to a thousand years or more, until the ice retreated far enough to the north to allow salt water to create Puget Sound, around 15,500 years ago. Genetic research shows that harbor seals may have used these lakes and their suitable habitat as a refuge during the Ice Age, and then evolved into a unique population of seals. I like to think that this is why they traverse the locks into the fresh water; they are simply playing out a life history deeply embedded in their DNA.

Birding at Sixty

I am not a big fan of driving, and there are probably some people who think I am somewhat obnoxious when I drive, but that's another story. I have found, though, that one way to pass the time is being observant. I watch out for speeders, speed traps, bad drivers, and the usual weather issues. I also keep a steady eye out for birds, in particular Red-tailed Hawks and Bald Eagles.

I am often rewarded. When I see one, I try to note it, usually with a pen at the ready and a tick mark on the back of my hand. I know that it's probably not the smartest thing I could do, but I have done it so often over the years, it's merely a moment's distraction. I have seen an average of 318 red-tails per year, mostly on I-5. (The 2022 Christmas Bird Count found 55 red-tails in the Seattle area, a new record for the count.)

Red-tails are not hard to spot. Sometimes they are flying, but more often they are perched on poles, branches, wires, bridges, and even the occasional street sign. It's always a bit of a surprise, and galvanizing, to see one just a few feet from the road, seemingly unbothered by multi-ton walls of death zooming past. Nor do they appear especially perturbed by crows, who regularly dive-bomb red-tails and are one of the best ways to spot the beautiful raptors.

On perches, red-tails often have a dark, football-shaped silhouette. They are about two-thirds the size of an eagle and quite a bit larger than crows and

Rock Pigeons, three other common freeway perchers. Red-tails have a mottled chest that looks almost like a bib, a small brown head, and a short tail. In flight, the two keys I look for are the red tail and patagial marks (from the Latin *patagium*, referring to the gold edging or border on a Roman woman's tunic), the dark bands at the front of the underside of the bird's wings.

When I reached out to raptor researcher Bud Anderson, he told me that "from here to Mexico, red-tails on freeways are seeking out voles." It's a pretty simple equation: Freeway medians are perfect vole habitat, and red-tails are programmed to eat voles. The problem, of course, is that a single-minded bird in pursuit of a meal does not stand a chance when hit by a vehicle. "Freeways are prey-rich tunnels of death," says Bud.

Sadly, red-tails are one of many birds dying along freeways. Owls die far more often: total carcass removal on Washington highways between 2015 and 2020 was 683 owls versus 278 raptors (of which 62 were identified as red-tails). Sarah Croston at the Washington State Department of Transportation says it's because "owls fly low when they are hunting, which makes them particularly susceptible to

vehicular strikes especially during crepuscular/nocturnal hours." Sarah and her colleague Glen Kalisz told me that not a lot can be done to avoid collisions, but Glen had some advice. "If you see an animal in the distance, slow down, pay attention to other drivers around you, and be prepared to react.... A couple extra seconds of reaction time can make a huge difference."

To me, it's the same message that I have been trying to write about for most of my career. Be aware. Pay attention. Slow down. In addition to Glen's advice, here are two more things you can do to help:

- If you want to report a dead bird, you can do so through the Birds Connect Seattle's dBird, a coast-to-coast collision reporting website (dbird.org), which is being used to help conservation work.
- We have a lot of rodents, but unfortunately, many popular poisons use anticoagulant rodenticides, which can bioaccumulate and cause problems in raptors. So don't use these evil chemicals.

When I see a Red-tailed Hawk, I am reminded of a line from *Watchable Birds of the Southwest* by Mary Taylor Gray: "The sight of a redtail is somehow reassuring—proof that there are still places wild enough for a hawk to exist." I guess that the interstate system must be wilder than I thought.

Otters in Our Midst

Nature abounds in the city, and where there's nature, there's poop. If one is lucky, one gets to seek it out and collect it, which I got to do on one warm September morning. What more could an urban naturalist want? I was with University of Washington PhD student Yasmine Hentati, who is collecting otter scat and using DNA sequencing to find out what the sleek mustelids are eating. Apex predators, the otters studied in other areas primarily eat fish, as well as crustaceans, amphibians, birds, and small mammals, which is probably what they eat here too. Yasmine also hopes to use the fecal samples to identify parasites and test for urban contaminants. By the way, the correct term for said product of the otter is *spraint*. Who knew? Now you do, about doo-doo.

Unlike what happened in many other places, it appears that pelt collectors did not extirpate the Puget Sound otter population, though they decimated the sea otter population outside the Sound. (Sea otters do not typically occur south of Admiralty Inlet—perhaps because of a lack of kelp beds, though biologists cannot say for sure—but apparently a lone male has lived down in Carr Inlet.) The main reason for Yasmine's study, which is partially funded by the Washington Department of Fish and Wildlife, is to provide basic information, such as population, diet, and home range (a male's range tends to be larger than a female's), for better management. Plus, she notes, knowing what the otters eat will help create a census of who else lives, and dies, around Seattle.

In contrast to many animals that cast their scats willy-nilly (derivation of the phrase *will he, nill he*, popularized by none other than Shakespeare in *Hamlet*), river otters tend to tidiness, concentrating their deposits in a relatively small space called a latrine, used most likely by a family group—mom and her offspring. This could be for social reasons (river otters are rather social), says Yasmine, but no one knows for sure. In order to find the latrines, she walked many miles along the city's saltwater and freshwater boundaries. (East Coast river otters live up to their name, sticking to freshwater habitat, whereas West Coast ones inhabit both.) River otters seem to like features in a landscape, such as a peninsula or river bend, but Yasmine found her best success at marinas. "This does not endear them to people, especially when

the otters poop on cleats or leave behind eviscerated birds." Otters also produce what is known as anal jelly (don't think too much about what it must look like), which Yasmine also collects because it contains additional DNA evidence not found in a spraint.

We collected at two marinas, Boat Street and Shilshole Bay. In both locations, the otters chose the wood docks over cement ones. At Boat Street, where otters had made life unpleasant for one boat owner, the owner had tried to discourage them with streamers, but still they pooped. "Looks like that otter had a bad day; it's a bit runny," noted Yasmine, with the sanguinity of a seasoned researcher. At Shilshole Bay, rain the previous night had partially disintegrated the spraints, which is not good because it leads to less available DNA. To collect the samples (#358 and #359), Yasmine picked them up with a resealable plastic bag; placed the package in a second, more secure bag; and used a marker to note the location, date, and estimated age of deposit.

Yasmine's study is not the first in Seattle. In 2022, Michelle Wainstein and colleagues published a report of river otters based on spraints collected along the Duwamish River from its lower Superfund stretch up into wilder areas (where it's called the Green River). They found very high concentrations of PCBs, polycyclic aromatic hydrocarbons (PAHs), polybrominated diphenyl ethers (PDBEs), and DDTs, exacerbated by bioaccumulation from the otters' food source, primarily fish. This study shows that our urban ecosystem is woefully polluted, says Michelle. But "I think perhaps of more interest is that river otters seem to be surprisingly resilient—surviving, persisting, and even reproducing despite having extremely high levels of toxic contaminants in their bodies. That's hopeful, but ideally not cause for complacency."

The urban environment is often overlooked as a place of wildness, where plants and animals live out their lives. Clearly, many do make their homes

SPRAINT

Otters are so cool that people have even created a specific name for the animal's poop. According to the *Oxford English Dictionary*, the word *spraint* has been around since 1425, when none other than the Duke of York wrote about it in *The Master of Game*. *Spraint* comes from the Old French *espraintes*, meaning "to squeeze out," and is cognate with our word *express* and the Latin *exprimere*, also meaning "to squeeze out." I did not make this up—one of the many reasons I love words. (And, despite what some say, *espresso*'s origins lay in making the drink on the spot, as opposed to it being squeezed, or pressed, out. Oh well.) What's unclear is why otters—beyond their coolness—merited this specific word for such a common thing.

with us, for better and for worse, for them and for us. As Michelle notes, we cannot simply sit back and watch when animals such as river otters, Bald Eagles, and coyotes thrive in our midst; we also should be vigilant and continue to work to make the urban world a healthier place for these animals. Doing so is not only good for us and them, but it's also simply a more equitable and fairer way to inhabit our home place.

A Celebration of Birds

I have no ear for birdsong and can identify only a handful of birds by their voice. I can never remember the various shorebirds, though I do love saying their names: Whimbrel, curlew, godwit, turnstone. Each lovely and melodic and evocative, but not memory triggering when it comes to identifying them. And, once, after telling what looked to be a serious birder—big binoculars, gaggle (hope you like the way I seeded a bird-related word in here) of bird books—that I had seen a particular species, he quite nicely informed me that I might want to reconsider my observation. (He didn't mention this, but I later learned that the bird I named was rarely found closer than several hundred miles from where I misspoke.)

But I am not here to crow about my incompetence. I write this essay to celebrate my past week of birding, when I was able to identify three members of the winged nation, in a very sort of Paul Reveresque manner: one by ear, two by sight. The first occurred in what I call birding by butt, which involves sitting and observing, preferably in a plush chair. (I think that with all the brouhaha about Big Year birding, when people set out to see as many bird species as they can in a single year, a Big Butt Bird Year could be quite popular: just sit, watch, and count.)

In my situation, I was sitting at our dining room table, drinking coffee and reading the newspaper, at 6:06 a.m. when I heard the very owl-like sound of *who*-ing. I knew that I had heard the sound before but could not remember who was *who*-ing. So I cheated. I used the amazing Merlin Bird ID app. If you are not aware of it, I highly recommend it. You hold up your phone, the app listens, and it tells you what you are hearing, though experienced birders will tell you that Merlin makes mistakes, so as with any electronic "facts" you get, be careful.

I was hearing a Barred Owl. According to Merlin, the owl was inquiring as to my household food situation: "Who cooks for you? Who cooks for you all?" My wife and I share that responsibility. Barred Owls are an über-owl with a round head, no ear tufts, large eyes, and a noticeable beak. They have a mottled brown-and-white feather pattern. My good friend, the eminent birder and artist Tony Angell, once shared his house with a Barred Owl and wrote in his beautiful book *The House of Owls* that Buttons was quite a charmer, allowing Tony to scratch his head and then returning the gesture and preening around Tony's ears.

Barred Owls are somewhat controversial. Originally a resident of the eastern United States, the species expanded their range to the west because of environmental changes wrought by settlement. The owls were first seen in western Washington in 1982 and subsequently have been cited as having a detrimental effect on Northern Spotted Owl populations. Barred Owls are now the most common owl in Seattle.

I actually had to get off my tush to see the other two birds. My wife and I were in Discovery Park on a lovely day. We were atop the bluff enjoying the view and looking at birds in the nearby trees when she noticed a large bird partially blocked by vegetation. Ever the gallant birder, I handed her my binoculars. She took a gander and discovered (hence the park's name) that she was seeing a Pileated Woodpecker. We rejoiced. Who wouldn't when seeing a rolling pin–sized, black-and-white bird with a red cap and a bill that looks as if it could penetrate concrete?

Pileateds are one of those birds more often interpreted to be present than actually encountered. That's because of the cavities they excavate in trees searching for ants, termites, and wood-boring insects. An early regional bird book described cavities measuring twenty-four by eight inches with depths of two to four inches. Cavity building helped give woodpeckers names such as hewel, hew-hole, and hickwall, whereas *pileated* comes from the Latin *pileus*, meaning "felt cap."

For our second exciting bird at Discovery Park, we saw the RuPaul of the avian world, a bird described in *Birds of America* as "shades of blending beauty, velvety black, brightening into fawn, melting browns, shifting saffrons, quaker drabs, pale blue, and slate with trimmings of white and golden yellow, and little red appendages on the wing." They even have a drag queen kind of name, Cedar Waxwing.

Our sighting at Discovery was a particularly nice and unexpected treat. We have been lucky to have an earful of Cedar Waxwings and their unique, high-pitched whistling as they flock to our front yard's black hawthorn (*Crataegus douglasii*) tree and feast on the berries. Berry eating defines the lifestyle of waxwings and was what we were seeing at Discovery Park, where their fruit of choice was from a madrona tree. Waxwings sometimes overindulge, though. If they eat too many fermented fruits, they can become intoxicated and occasionally obnoxious. Just one more reason to like these lovely birds.

Although most weeks in Seattle do not reward my birding endeavors as this one did, I always keep my eyes and ears open for our avian residents and visitors. They are the one group of animals that I see or hear every single day, forever delighting me and connecting me to the wilder world around me. I am sure that I misidentify them on occasion, but I am okay with that, and I know they don't care.

Flying Rats, or Models of Evolution

A small gang lives in my neighborhood. Like most gangs, the members look alike; slate-gray and green dominate the color scheme. They like to hang out by the corner telephone pole. Sometimes they burst into one of my neighbors' yards and harass them. They don't hurt anyone, but they can be troublesome. I am not bothered by this gang. I am in the minority; most people dislike these pigeons.

They say that pigeons are dirty birds, that they mob backyard bird feeders and steal the food from "more worthy" birds. They say the pigeons don't belong in our quiet neighborhood. They want to rid the local park of what have been called "rats with wings."

Rumor has it that pigeons—or Rock Pigeons, as birders officially call them—reached the Seattle area within days of the first pioneer's arrival. This is rather hard to prove, but pigeons are omnipresent in the Emerald City. (Pigeon Point in West Seattle may be named for our local pigeon, the Band-tailed Pigeon.) Seattle is not unique in this avian invasion. Native to Europe, Africa, and Asia, pigeons nest, eat, and procreate on five continents. The earliest North American records are from 1606 in Port Royal, Nova Scotia.

We, of course, can blame no one but ourselves. Humans have customized cities for pigeons. Our propensity for dropping edible morsels provides plenty of food for the birds. We build deep chasms of buildings that simulate pigeons' native habitat of canyons with numerous clefts for housing (hence *Rock* Pigeon). We even construct buildings that offer prime nesting sites: small, well-protected ledges.

Despite our dislike for the bird, they have many admirable qualities. In addition to being good providers, urban pigeons are models of fidelity. Unlike some urban dwellers, pairing for life is the norm for pigeons. This may occur because the birds are sedentary, constantly together, and able to reproduce year-round. Some people believe that pigeons must emerge fully grown because they have never seen a young pigeon. This is not true; the young just have good parents, who feed and watch over their progeny, known as a squab, until they are large enough to fledge.

What we consider to be an ungainly animal can fly faster than most big-league pitchers can throw a baseball. Homing pigeons, trained to take advantage of the bird's speed and navigational skills, have been used for over two thousand years. They carried news of Caesar's conquest of Gaul back to Rome. After Napoleon's defeat at Waterloo, a pigeon carrying the news beat a horse and rider back to London by four days. The Maidenform company even made pigeon vests during World War II for US paratroopers; after landing, they would release the birds to carry secret messages back to headquarters.

Pigeons also learn from one another. In one study, four birds were trained to obtain food by poking a hole into a paperboard feed box. After returning the birds to their old haunts, the researchers tracked the spread of the new skill. Within a month, twenty-four other birds had mastered the technique.

Another attribute we may fail to credit is the bird's vacuuming ability. When we see pigeons eating those discarded hot dogs, sandwiches, or

cookies, we should realize that the birds help keep the urban world a cleaner place and prevent the food from ending up in the mouths of true rats. Sure, pigeons produce prodigious quantities of their own waste, but at least deposition is generally concentrated around their nesting spots.

We can also credit pigeons for playing a key role in one of the most important ideas ever proposed: natural selection. In the first chapter of *On the Origin of Species*, Charles Darwin wrote, "Believing that it is always best to study some special group, I have, after deliberation, taken up domestic pigeons." He raised them, collected their skins to study, and joined two pigeon clubs in London. His studying was not for idle curiosity but served a purpose; Darwin thought that human manipulation of pigeons could be looked at as analogous to natural selection. Breeders chose certain attributes in a pigeon that they liked and bred the birds to try to produce an animal that always showed those features. Over time, this type of selection led to a new breed. Pigeons, therefore, exemplified "natural selection," even if humans controlled it.

An argument has been made for other urban species, such as starlings and dandelions, that we often denigrate those most like us. Like us, pigeons are adaptable, reproductively successful, and cosmopolitan. Perhaps we should grant them more respect. After all, Charles Darwin appreciated them, and he knew a bit more about the natural world than the average person.

Woolly Dogs

Seattleites are notoriously poochophilic. The 2020 census showed that the city's residents have more dogs than children, 153,000 to 107,178. And in 2019, a Rover and Redfin report ranked Seattle as the number one most dog-friendly city. This is not the first time outsiders have noted the region's dogs.

Sailing down Puget Sound on May 24, 1792, Captain George Vancouver wrote in his journal of an abundance of dogs that "were all shorn as close to the skin as sheep are in England . . . and were composed of a mixture of a coarse kind of wool, with very fine long hair, capable of being spun into yarn." He thought they resembled Pomeranians, but in fact, they were a unique breed specific to the Salish Sea and long known in Lushootseed as ske'-ha and more recently known in English as Coast Salish woolly dogs. A few weeks later, Vancouver wrote that Mr. Whidbey had observed about two hundred Native people "walking along the shore [of what is now Camano Island, north of Whidbey Island], attended by about forty dogs in a drove." These dogs were also shorn.

Forty-nine years later, when the US Exploring Expedition sailed down the Sound, Coast Salish woolly dogs also attracted the attention of the crew. One noted that dogs were domesticated and numerous, and another observed blankets made of dog hair. The first high-quality image came from Canadian artist Paul Kane, who painted the dogs in 1847 and wrote that they had "long hair of a brownish black and a clear white." Adding to the unique and special status of Coast Salish woolly dogs, the only other group of Native people in the Americas to domesticate an animal in order to use their hair for spinning wool for textiles were ancient Peruvians, who used alpaca and llama.

Unfortunately, Coast Salish woolly dogs went extinct in the late 1800s, and only one pelt, that of a dog named Mutton, exists. He was the companion of naturalist and ethnographer George Gibbs, who obtained him in 1858 or 1859 somewhere around the Salish Sea. Like many dogs, Mutton was an opportunist; in 1859, he ate the head off a mountain goat specimen that had been given to Gibbs by another naturalist, Dr. Caleb Kennerly. In response, "Mutton was sheared a short time ago, & as soon as his hair grows out we will make a specimen of him," wrote Kennerly to the Smithsonian's Spencer Baird on August 19, 1859.

SALISH

The word refers to both a family of languages and to ethnically related people who speak the language. *Salish* came into English from the Bitterroot Salish people of Montana, who called themselves Séliš, or "the people." More than two dozen distinct languages and many dialects comprise the family, which is separated into Coastal Salish (Vancouver Island to northwest Oregon) and Interior Salish, stretching to eastern Montana.

Mutton's mortal remains sat—overlooked and mostly forgotten—in a drawer at the Smithsonian until researchers Candace Wellman and Russel Barsh separately tracked him down in 2002. Then, in 2021, Audrey Lin, an evolutionary molecular biologist at the Smithsonian, learned about Mutton. "I had heard from some other people that he was a bit scraggly, but I thought he was gorgeous," she told me. Audrey also learned that no one had ever made an extensive study of the pelt.

Teaming up with a diverse group of researchers, including First Nations and Tribal members whose ancestors had long kept woolly dogs, Audrey began a genetic and cultural study of Mutton. In late 2023, the researchers published their study of Mutton in *Science*. Genetically similar to precontact dogs from Newfoundland and British Columbia, woolly dogs diverged from other breeds as long as 4,776 years ago, about the time they appeared in the archaeological record. The team also produced a drawing of Mutton, the first one of a Coast Salish woolly dog based on actual remains. He looked like a combination of a Finnish spitz and a Samoyed.

The ongoing collaboration between researchers and Indigenous people continues to illustrate how the Pacific Northwest's long-term residents maintained a sustainable, integrated, and reciprocal relationship with their natural environment. The research also reveals a fundamental aspect of dogs: that long ago, they figured us out and realized that people could be domesticated to aid dogs and make them happy with food and shelter. I, for one, am glad they did. Woof woof.

Scolding Crows

Late spring 'tis the season when crows are out and about protecting their youngsters and their nests. I got to experience this on one of my runs. I was minding my own business, heading down an alley, when I heard squawking and wings flapping as a crow skirted my head. The bird landed on a fence, scolded me for bothering his or her territory, and then flew up to buzz me again, and again, and again. Finally, I reached the end of the bird's territory and continued my run in peace.

This was not the first time a crow had decided what my big brother thought in our youth—that I was in the wrong place and needed to be reminded of the error of my ways. Fortunately, the crow didn't whack me in the head, as others have experienced, but it was still unnerving to have the bird clearly bothered by my presence and descend in pursuit of my noggin.

I can only imagine how the hawks feel. One day while driving down I-5 from Arlington, I spotted three Red-tailed Hawks at different locations because crows were dive-bombing the raptors. This is not unusual, but what stood out is that nearly all my sightings occurred because of the agitated maneuvering of the corvids. Infants in the nest probably made the crows more active and more diligent in harassing the hawks; however, red-tails are far more interested in small mammals than baby birds, though they might take one or two opportunistically. Crows also regularly buzz Bald Eagles, and for good reason; eagles often attack and kill crow nestlings and fledglings.

Crows may also mob people and other predators for another reason. In their fine book, *In the Company of Crows and Ravens*, John Marzluff and Tony Angell discuss studies where jays and crows seemingly seek out a predator specifically to harass. The authors write that experimental evidence suggests that the corvids are "in fact advertising their self-worth!" When given an opportunity to attack a mounted Eurasian Eagle-Owl surrounded by mounted crows, the wild crows not only mobbed the owl but also the ersatz crows. "In fact, they attacked the [mounted] crows more often than the owl when the experiment was conducted in common flocking areas, where advertising one's self worth is likely to reap the greatest social benefit." And you wonder why people tend to anthropomorphize animals... or maybe we are simply emulating them.

Over the past two decades, Marzluff has conducted several studies testing crow mobbing behavior. In one study, the focus was whether the crows perceived threatening people, defined as a masked person trapping crows with a net launcher. The birds clearly didn't forget a face. No matter the age, ethnicity, size, or style of gait of the person wearing the mask of the trapper, the crows recognized the face, became agitated, and mobbed the person. A second study then showed that crows spread the word about the so-called dangerous face of the despised trapper; in the years following the initial trapping, the percentage of crows scolding people with a mask similar to the trapper's face increased from 30 to 66 percent. The conclusion: young crows learned to scold from their parents. And you wonder why people tend to anthropomorphize animals.

Despite the seasonal mobbing by crows, I am a huge fan of them. I like how they are so interactive with the world around them. They respond to

others. They care for their family members. They gather together for their dead. They teach. They make tools. They make fools . . . of us. They problem solve. They have fun. They banter. And they are enjoyable to watch.

If you want to see crows in all their splendor, the best spot in the region is the University of Washington's Bothell campus, where more than fifteen thousand crows roost together in the winter. There are fewer crows in the summer because most are out on nests breeding and mobbing those who venture too close, including one runner in one alley.

Little Red Fish of Lake Sammamish

One mid-November, I had the good fortune of watching an unusual group of salmon head up a small tributary of Lake Sammamish. I was on private land on the east side of the lake, and dozens upon dozens of kokanee were swimming up the creek. The females were searching for a spot to deposit their eggs, and the males were battling to be part of the reproductive cycle. It was amazing, hopeful, and exciting to see these lovely fish return to waters that they have been visiting for thousands of years. Isolated during the last Ice Age from kokonee in Lake Washington, the Lake Sammamish fish evolved into a genetically distinct population different from their cousins in the larger lake.

A variety of sockeye salmon that does not migrate, kokanee spend their entire lives in fresh water. Indigenous people and early settlers considered the "little red fish," as they are sometimes called, the region's best-tasting salmon. An 1893 advertisement in a local newspaper listed kokanee trout for sale at a quarter a pound; halibut was a dime, and salmon was 12.5 cents a pound. Kokanee were further valued because they returned to their birth streams later in the year than other salmon species.

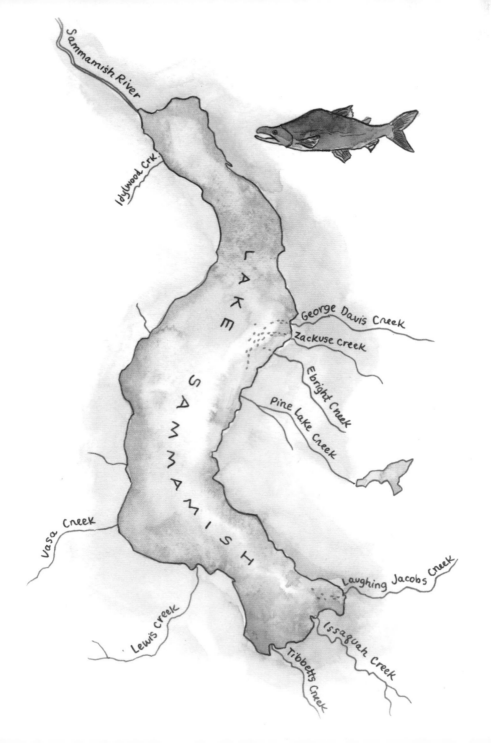

KOKANEE

The name comes from kəkn̓iʔ, the n̓saȋxčin̓ (Colville-Okanagan Salish) word for landlocked salmon. Before the name was commonly accepted for the fish, there were the SS *Kokanee* (a steamer built in 1896), Kokanee Creek, and a mountain range, the latter two in British Columbia. Pre-1900 references to this fish around Seattle called them redfish, silver trout, and Kennerly's salmon. The name *kokanee* didn't come into popular usage until the 1940s, and even then, few people used it or knew anything about the fish's life history.

As happened with salmon populations in many locations, and many other plant and animal species, the local kokanee runs plummeted during the twentieth century. Historically, habitat loss, pollutants, and urbanization all played a role, as did the introduction of sockeye, Chinook, and steelhead, as well as bass and perch (aggressive, non-native fish) beginning in the 1890s. More recent challenges include scoured stream beds due to impermeable concrete and asphalt creating greater flow rates and a stratified water column of too-warm water on the top and too little oxygen deeper down, locally called "the squeeze," because it restricts where kokanee can live.

Despite these many issues, kokanee have been returning recently to several tributaries of Lake Sammamish, including Ebright, Laughing Jacobs, George Davis, and Zackuse Creeks. All of these creeks and the surrounding land are part of the traditional land of the Snoqualmie people, who relied on kokanee as central to their diet and still consider the fish to be an important cultural resource.

Part of what made the kokanee runs I saw so stunning and hopeful is that their return is due in part to a group of people focused on the fish and their health. These people have worked to restore habitat (one homeowner personally paid to remove a pipe that blocked fish passage), replace culverts, develop micro-hatcheries (called remote stream incubators), monitor the streams and the fish, and educate others.

Recently, Jeff Jensen, a fisheries biologist at the University of Washington Bothell, who has been involved with the Lake Sammamish fish, made another important and exciting discovery: kokanee inhabiting Lake Washington. Based on DNA studies, Jeff has shown that the fish are true native Lake Washington kokanee, which had long been thought to be extirpated. Because there's a small chance they aren't, Jeff hopes to run a DNA test on kokanee collected at a Lake Washington tributary in 1888–1889. (I just have to write that doing a DNA test on fish dead for more than a century is darned, wicked cool.)

Biologists such as Jeff don't know if the high-quality return was an aberration or a trend. Either way, it is positive and an illustration that each of us can make a difference in helping to create a better place for all who live here.

Clam Slamming

On our way up to Anacortes to catch the ferry to Shaw and Lopez Islands, my wife and I stopped at the Tommy Thompson Trail in Anacortes. The trail runs along an old train track for 3.3 miles. We had limited time, so we headed to the section that crosses the restored train trestle across Fidalgo Bay. Built around 1891, the trestle linked Anacortes to the east, at Weaverling Spit, which facilitated the movement of goods and people.

What interested me were the Glaucous-winged Gulls and their use of the trail as a sort of molluscan nutcracker. Our first signs of how the birds took advantage of the hard surface, which was mostly wood slats, were the broken clam shells. We didn't see any birds at first, but then we saw a gull fly over, hover slightly, and drop a clam, which didn't break. To our surprise, the gull picked the clam back up and dropped it again.

For decades, ornithologists have described this curious behavior of gulls. One study conducted in the San Juan Islands and at Seattle's Golden Gardens Park found "an age-related progression of increased clam-slamming efficiency," or what is also called learned behavior. As birds get older, experience leads to them dropping clams from higher heights, adjusting their drop height based on the object's weight, and choosing harder substrates, such as parking lots and railroad trestles, instead of mudflats. They also tend to fumble fewer airborne clams and are more efficient in choosing clams that are relatively easier to break and provide more meat. In scientific speak, "discrimination of profitable prey sizes takes longer to perfect," another group of clam slam researchers wrote.

At least nine species of gulls take advantage of gravity and Newton's laws of thermodynamics to obtain a meal. Or as a friend explained the science of the clam drops to me:

> *The clam of a particular mass has a particular gravitational potential energy based on its height. As the clam drops, the clam gains kinetic energy based on its mass and acceleration, minus the losses as friction heats the air; it loses gravitational potential energy as height goes to zero. Upon impact, the kinetic energy is converted into heat in a variety of ways, like bouncing, bending, or breaking the clam on the ground, or heating the air with sound waves, unless it bounces up onto a rock, in which case some of the kinetic energy is converted back into gravitational potential energy. The impact force is calculated using Newton's second law, and because of Newton's third law, the ground acts as a hammer with an equal and opposite force on the clam.*

The other group of gravity-exploiting birds is the corvid family of ravens, rooks, jays, and crows. In one study of crows, the crows acted similarly to gulls but went a step further by adjusting their drop height in relation to how many times they had dropped the walnut. In other words, the birds realized that they were weakening the walnut shell and didn't need to spend the energy to reach the original drop height. They also lowered drop height if other crows who might steal a meal were nearby; being lower to the ground increased the likelihood of eating the meal they were preparing. (So, honey, what are you doing today? Oh, just going out to watch crows drop walnuts. Ah, the life of a scientist!)

But, as in any situation, sometimes bad things can happen when animals exploit gravity. Legend has it that the fifth-century BCE Greek poet of tragedies, Aeschylus, died because an eagle or a vulture known as a lammergeier mistook the poet's bald pate for a rock and dropped a turtle on him. Ironically, according to Pliny the Elder, Aeschylus was outside that day because "an oracle, it is said, had predicted his death on that day by the fall of a house." So, friends, be careful out there.

Terror of the Docks

Few animals struck as much fear into early Seattleites as what the *Seattle Times* once called the "terror of the dock builder." Known as shipworms, they were actually clams that looked like a worm sporting a conical helmet. The clams used this shell to drill into the thousands of pilings placed along the waterfront, converting them to a Swiss cheese texture, which typically resulted in their failure. For example, the Seattle and Walla Walla Railroad trestle I described in "When Fill Fails" was rendered useless within a year of its completion because of teredo clams (another name for the bivalve), and two port commission laborers ended up in the water when a different trestle-supported railroad pier collapsed.

For at least two thousand years, ravenous mollusks have eaten their way through human-made wood structures in salt water around the world. This was particularly common in the Mediterranean Sea, where they were well known for their ability to sink ships and inspire writers, such as the Roman poet Ovid, who wrote, "'Tis then no marvel if my heart has softened and melts as water runs from snow. It is gnawed as a ship is injured by the hidden borer." Now that's some misery.

Here in Puget Sound, our species is *Bankia setacea*. (Another well-known species is the non-native *Teredo navalis*, but they are generally found more to the south.) Like other saltwater clams, they have minute, free-swimming larvae, which eventually land on wood and begin to burrow, trending parallel to the grain of the wood. *Bankia* can grow up to three feet long with a shell width slightly less than an inch. As they burrow and honeycomb their home, they feed via a pair of siphons that extend out of their front-door entry. When threatened, they withdraw the siphons and plug the hole with feather-like structures called pallets, which tend to hide the destruction within.

Found across the Sound, shipworms were notorious for their ability to reduce solid, old-growth pilings to frail, ransacked logs of little worth. "Led by their trusty commander, Voracious Appetite, unnumbered battalions of the Teredinidae nation have invaded Salmon Bay," wrote a *Seattle Times* reporter on June 11, 1915. But not everyone disliked them; a January 6, 1888, article in the *San Francisco Bulletin* quoted a retired sea captain who noted how the clams helped eliminate drifting logs and floating wrecks that could damage ships: "It is a part of his business to clear the high seas of wreckage, so that there shall be fewer perils for ships and human life." How could anyone abhor an animal so devoted to aiding our species in times of peril?

Apparently many did, and they launched a toxic attack to stop the clam. Lumber mills tried soaking logs in creosote, coal tar, asbestos, castor oil, and strychnine, but the poisons apparently "pleased the teredo much, seeming to act

SOUND

Cartographers do not have a specific definition for a sound, though some have favored its use for a channel that can easily be sounded. British explorer George Vancouver gave us the name when he honored his lieutenant Peter Puget in May 1792 with Puget's Sound. He could have also used *gulf* or *bay* for the waterway. *Sound* comes from both the Old English *sund*, meaning "water" or "sea," and the Old Norse *sund*, meaning "swimming" or "strait." It seems to be a place-name primarily used by the British, including writers such as John Milton and Jonathan Swift.

as a condiment on what must have been a rather monotonous bill of fare," wrote a *Portland Oregonian* correspondent in 1891. Another method was to use pilings still covered in bark. During the growing season, workers would girdle the bark just above the base, which killed the tree, and then let the bark shrink for several months before cutting it and using it as a piling.

Lest you think that shipworms and other similar wood-damaging invertebrates no longer strike fear into maritime planners and engineers, you would be mistaken. Ironically, such worries are a relatively recent manifestation. During the decades when industrialization contaminated urban marine waterways, the teredo clam problem disappeared primarily because the clams couldn't tolerate the pollution. Now that urban waters are cleaner, teredo clams have returned, and the hungry bivalves have again started to eat away at old pilings.

Seattle has felt the modern influence of shipworms. One of the reasons that the city worked to replace its aging seawall between 2013 and 2017 was damage to the wood substructure caused by the teredo clams and other marine borers called gribbles. For the new seawall, builders avoided wood and relied on materials less susceptible to invertebrates.

I suspect that we may not ever stop the shipworms. Paleontologists have found traces of shipworm activity in twenty- to thirty-five-million-year-old fossilized wood in sandstones from Puget Sound and on the Olympic Peninsula. Boring into and eating wood is clearly a successful way of life, which has persisted for millions of years and will most likely continue long into the future. Perhaps we simply need to take the long view and learn to live with these ancient terrors.

Horsepower

The term *horsepower* today is commonly used to refer to the power an engine produces. In Seattle's early days, that engine was equine. Street trolleys, fire engines, wagons, and carts were some of the 3,945 horse-drawn vehicles noted in a traffic count on December 23, 1904, at the corner of Second Avenue and Pike Street; there were fourteen automobiles. All of those horses had to be housed somewhere. According to *Polk's Seattle City Directory*, at least seventeen public livery, sale, and boarding stables dotted the urban landscape in 1890, with a peak of thirty-seven in 1910.

I know of only three remaining in the city but suspect there are others. The oldest was built in 1902 as the Rainier Boarding and Livery Stable. Located on Western Avenue, it housed a bike shop from 1983 to 2014 and now has a brewery. Next younger is the C. B. Van Vorst Building at 415 Boren Avenue North. Built in 1909, it had room for 250 horses, mostly used by one of Seattle's long-loved institutions, the Frederick & Nelson department store. Although designated a City of Seattle Landmark in 2000, the structure was mostly altered via a facademy, which left behind just the facade of the original building.

My favorite—and the lone one that passersby might suspect has an equine connection—is a block north of the old Rainier Stable. The Union Stables

opened in 1910 and had room for three hundred horses, which could access the upper floors of the five-story building via an internal ramp. What makes the building my favorite is the big horse head mounted high on the facade. It is a clear sign of who used to be the priority inside the building.

Other links to Seattle's horse-powered past can be found around the city. Up on Capitol Hill along 14th Avenue—often called Millionaire's Row—are two reminders: hitching posts and stepping stones. At the former home of Elbridge Amos Stuart, the man who started the Carnation Evaporated Milk Company, is a granite block where a rider or passenger could place a foot when disembarking. Around the corner is a hitching post, and another stepping stone is a couple blocks north.

Over the years, I have located several others. A bit south of Mr. Stuart's equine stones are two more granite hitching posts, one of which shows up on a 1910 postcard of the street. Two are on 22nd Avenue East, near Prospect Street, another is in front of the Frye Art Museum and came from the home of Charles and Emma Frye, and one is on the southwest corner of Minor Avenue and James Street. There are also two hitching posts, or structures that look very similar to one, on Queen Anne Hill. One is where Fifth Avenue West and West Kinnear Place curve together, and the second is slightly east, where the two roads split.

When I asked historian Fred Brown, who wrote *The City Is More Than Human*, about the posts, he told me that it was illegal to have animals running at large in early Seattle. If they strayed and were caught by city-hired herders, they ended up in the cattle pound. He further told me that the Humane Society pushed for laws that required teamsters to carry weights they could attach to horses to keep them from running wild and injuring pedestrians or themselves. Tying a horse to a hitching post was a simple solution to these issues.

I am pleased to see that a modern form of the hitching post has begun to crop up around the city. Our neighbors recently installed a black metal post equipped with a power cable. It's a charger for their electric cars. From hitching post to gas pump to power post, technology marches on, always finding a new source of horsepower.

The Hub in the Wheel of the Sound

Few events exemplify Puget Sound's many circles of life as abundantly as a herring spawn. The excitement begins when male herring start pumping out milt that can be so prodigious it turns the water a creamy turquoise. In response, females release between ten thousand to forty-five thousand eggs per fish, which settle and stick on seagrass, where fertilization occurs. During massive spawning events, millions of fish are involved, and then, several weeks later, the fish migrate back to their normal feeding grounds, either elsewhere in the Sound or out in the open ocean.

Such events have been magnets of life for thousands of years. For the Indigenous people of the Whulge (the Native name for Puget Sound) and the Salish Sea, the great schools of herring were essential, not simply because of the vast numbers of fish but also because of the timing when the herring returned. Adult fish began to arrive in late winter and early spring and provided valuable meat and oil at a time when other foods weren't as available. In addition, the birds and mammals attracted to the herring likely provided further resources. Hungry visitors would have included animals such as wolves, humpback whales, bears, seals, Bald Eagles, porpoises, and deer.

WHULGE

The oldest place-name we have for our inland waterway, x̌ʷəlč —often writ-ten in English as *whulge*—means "salt water" and is the Lushootseed word for Puget Sound. I have been told that it is derived from the noise that waves make as they come up on the beach. To the Native people, who had few names for large geographic features, x̌ʷəlč is more of a concept than a defined location; it's a way to delineate a relationship to place for the waterway's Coast Salish people, as in "We are of the salt water."

Animals seek out these teeming schools because herring "are really good at eating tiny, crunchy things and converting them into delicious fatty meals," as one biologist told me. Herring are first-level consumers; they vacuum up detritus and phytoplankton, or microalgae, and in turn, get eaten by sec-ondary consumers. In this role between the lower and higher levels of the food chain, herring connect everything in Puget Sound, says Ole Shelton, a National Oceanic and Atmospheric Administration ecologist. "They con-nect the open ocean to the coast. They link predator and prey. They transmit nutrients between ecosystems. They are very much the hub in the wheel of the Sound."

As I described in my book *Homewaters*, I was fortunate to witness two spawning events. The first was at Alki Point, where I joined my pal Lyanda Lynn Haupt to watch rafts of Surf Scoters, with their lovely black bodies, white head patches, and colorful bills. They would periodically disappear beneath the surface, descending in search of eggs, and then pop up like corks and rest on the surface to eat. The highlight was seeing a flying fish, or at least an adult herring, passing over us in the talons of an Osprey. But then the

Osprey returned back over the water, followed by a Bald Eagle. The Osprey soon dropped the fish, and the eagle abandoned her pursuit of the Osprey and seemed ready to dive into the water for the herring, but ultimately changed her mind and flew away.

The second spawning event I witnessed occurred on Hood Canal at Right Smart Cove, about six miles south and two coves west from a beach in Quilcene Bay known to the Skokomish people of Hood Canal as "landing for herring," a reference to its importance as a spawning ground. On the water were several hundred scaups, Surf Scoters, Buffleheads, American Wigeons, and goldeneyes. Another raft a quarter mile south was less diverse, almost all Surf Scoters, but larger, with what looked to be well over a thousand birds.

On the beach, my wife and I found eggs that had washed ashore and formed small piles up to fifteen feet long, several feet wide, and four to five inches deep. In the water that swirled in a small eddy, the eggs were so thick that the water had the consistency and color of watery Malt-O-Meal, though I assume the eggs taste better than the cereal to those hordes who descend to eat the nuggets of energy. Digging my hands into the piles, I scooped up a football-sized mass and could see many tiny eyes. So cute but sadly also destined to die, as few eggs that wash ashore can survive being out of water.

Luckily for those in Puget Sound, we have many opportunities to witness the spawning season. It typically begins in January, in Wollochet Bay, Quartermaster Harbor, and Port Orchard, and continues through the end of June, at Cherry Point. Over the past few years, Hood Canal has been the best place to experience big events, which attract stunning numbers of birds such as I saw. Go check it out.

A Singular Slug

The white, two-story house looks like many others in the tony Seattle neighborhood of Laurelhurst: understated and elegant with a well-cared-for yard. Few who walk by would guess that a notorious beast dwelt there until June 24, 1933, when California naturalist Tracey Storer caught a several-inch-long slug and took the specimen south. Storer's animal, known scientifically as *Arion rufus*, now rests in ethanol at the California Academy of Sciences.

For those who inhabit Seattle, or nearly any city between Arcata, California, and Vancouver, British Columbia, finding an *Arion rufus* in their yards would not prompt them to collect and preserve the slimy crawler at a leading scientific institution. Most people would probably kill the slug on the spot, or, if they were feeling generous, they might scoop up the offending gastropod and transfer the slippery mollusk out of their yards. The difference between now and then is that modern urbanites see *A. rufus*—also known to malacologists by the yummy dessert-sounding name of chocolate arion—as a good-for-nothing garden despoiler. Instead, Storer saw the slug as an unusual individual, singular by living and dying in Seattle; the one he collected is the first known specimen of this European native ever found in the western United States.

Initially discovered in this country in Detroit in 1912 and described as "a striking and beautiful object," *A. rufus* do not do well in cold climates. In contrast, the temperate, wet conditions of the Pacific Northwest allowed the slugs to became a pest in Seattle by 1940, followed within a decade or so by Oregon; Vancouver, British Columbia; and California. University of Washington biologist Eugene Kozloff summed up many people's feelings about *A. rufus* when he wrote in *Plants and Animals of the Pacific Northwest*, "If you have to hate anything, let it be this slug, a cruelly destructive pest if there ever was one." That seems a bit harsh to me; after all, they are only eating your vegetables.

Plus, like all animals, they have some rather nifty adaptations. When attacked, they shrink into a ball, rock from side to side, and cover themselves in slime. Although the mucus gums up the mouth of most attackers and prevents them from getting a grip, it is useless against another non-native, the great gray slug. In this situation, *A. rufus* tries to speed away, hoping that

the great gray attacks the slime puddle. If the attacker doesn't fall for this stunt, the chocolate arion is doomed; the speedy grays can quickly chase down a lumbering, soon-to-be meal. Those dead slugs you encounter on the pavement in the morning may be the result of slug-on-slug predation and not too much sun.

According to the splendid *Land Snails and Slugs of the Pacific Northwest* by Thomas E. Burke, at least twenty-nine species of slugs occur in Washington. Many, including twelve invaders from Europe, inhabit urban areas. A dozen years ago, I was lucky enough to hold one of the most beautiful natives, the blue-gray taildropper. What made the experience exciting and memorable was that the slug lived up to their (they are hermaphrodites, so *they/their* pronouns seem appropriate) name. When I looked away and then back again, two slugs, or at least one slug and their recently autotomized tail, nestled on my palm. We also have seven species of jumping-slugs, some of which can become airborne. They accomplish this feat via twitching; sadly, I haven't seen this.

Not everyone, however, is so quick to rise up against slugs. After hearing about the infamous slug collected by Tracey Storer, the home's current owner, a gardener, told me, "I guess I will have to be kinder and gentler to them."

Not-So-Silent Spring

Coming home late one day, I was startled by sound as I crossed I-5 on a pedestrian bridge north of our house. Of course, there was the mellifluous rhythm of traffic, but rising above that din was a sonic riot of Pacific tree frogs, also known as Pacific chorus frogs. They have the classic *ribb-it* or *krr-r-r-eek* call of a wild batrachian in love, or at least interested in mating. It's so classic, it's often the sound one hears for any type of frog in a movie, regardless of the location. (Red-tailed Hawks are the avian equivalent, the sound of nearly every bird of prey in a movie.)

These handsome frogs produce several types of calls. The mating call serves not only to attract females, who then base their mate selection on the call, but also to alert other males to the caller's space. If that space is invaded, then the call changes to an encounter, or staccato, call. If the intruder fails to acknowledge his adversary's warning, the two rivals bounce toward each other and whack each other's vocal sac with their own. Continuing to staccato call, with legs flailing, the two then try to deflate the other's sac. Whoever suffers the indignity of deflation then swims away.

Impressed and pleased as I was to hear the call of Pacific chorus frogs over the noise of the interstate, I know that they are affected by our aural emissions. Studies show a negative effect, with lowered reproductive success, increased physiological stress, and altered migration patterns. There doesn't seem to be an end to how we can mess with our fellow inhabitants of planet Earth.

Spring also brings other sounds to my ears, such as the chattering, squawks, and squalls of the Steller's Jay. These big blue birds, with their Elvish (the King, not the mythological kind) hairstyle, are forever making a brouhaha. As ornithologist Elliott Coues wrote in *Birds of the Northwest* in 1874, "They fret and scold about trifles, quarrel over anything, and keep everything in a ferment when they are about." But as many have also written, Steller's Jays are so splendidly captivating that our forests—urban and wild—would lose their vivacity without the bird's cacophony of observations and concerns, so I never mind their sounds. (*Steller* in their name honors Georg Wilhelm

Steller, who explored the northern Pacific with Vitus Bering—apparently he was the Strait guy of the pair.)

Then there are Red-winged Blackbirds; noisy, territorial, and garnished by vivid red epaulettes, they can be heard chattering with their distinctive *conk-la-ree* calls. They are also denizens of watery locales, where males flaunt their garish shoulder patches as a sign of territoriality. Studies have shown that if the birds intend to fight and protect their turf, they will display their badges of red, but if they are merely visiting or testing a new territory, they may not display, and instead wait to see what the present owner does. Seems a good lesson to learn: Be patient and sport red epaulettes, but only flare them when necessary. Otherwise, chill out.

In the first few weeks of spring, you can also find me thrilling to the trilling of Varied Thrushes. These orange-necked, black-bibbed cousins of robins typically start calling at dawn in a haunting, monotone whistle suffused with the mysteries of a mountain forest. Summer residents of higher elevation, they migrate down to hang out with we lowland dwellers from late fall to spring. The trilling notes feel not only like a rejoicing of spring but also a call to turn one's thoughts to the mountains.

With no disrespect to Rachel Carson, I didn't actually write this essay to honor the sounds of spring that she helped perpetuate. What I really wanted to discuss is the book *Sounds Wild and Broken* by David George Haskell. He is revelatory in his explorations of what he calls "part of the world's richness . . . the diversity of aural *experience*."

Reading David's book got me thinking about the long history of sound. Whenever we hear wind or rain, rockfall or lightning, ocean waves or water rushing, we are hearing noises little changed over the past 4.5 billion years. A landslide on early Earth sounded like one that fell yesterday. In stark contrast, the frogs' *ribbit*s near I-5, the jay's *shaack-shaack-shaack* in our backyard, or any of the other uncountable sounds produced by organic means are recent developments. The earliest fossil evidence for a sound-making structure is merely 270 million years old. Let me rephrase that: 94 percent of our planet's history passed before sonic communication began.

The evidence of first sound comes from an enigmatic, cricket-like insect, *Permostridulus brongniarti*, that lived in the middle of the supercontinent of Pangaea. Described in a 2003 paper in the *European Journal of Entomology*, the insect had a "bow of fused cross-veins . . . interpreted as a stridulatory apparatus." By rubbing their wings together, the insects produced an audible rasp, and biological singing was born.

Another 140 million years or so would pass before the true sonic revolution blossomed on land. The reason: flowering plants. Their rapid diversification led to a corresponding evolution of insect species and their chorus of sounds. The other great songsters of the planet—birds—didn't add their sonic repertoire until after sixty-six million years ago, following the great Cretaceous-Paleogene extinction, which also killed off the dinosaurs. (Despite what Hollywood would have us believe, dinosaurs were not aural communicators; they may have produced some windy utterances but not the emotive sounds popularized by the *Jurassic Park* movies.) Around 160 million years ago saw the evolution of the mammalian ear, which allowed our predecessors to hear high frequencies, but what sounds they produced, we know not, and that diversity only exploded after the Cretaceous-Paleogene extinction. Organic ocean sound began around two hundred million years ago.

We are indeed blessed that such a stimulating palette of sounds enriches our planet and our lives. But as David warns, we are facing a potential crisis. Not only are many of us estranged and disconnected from this sensory world, but we are also failing to recognize what we are missing. "When the most powerful species on Earth ceases to listen to the voices of others, calamity ensues. The vitality of the world depends, in part, on whether we turn our ears back to the living Earth." Two fine steps in doing so: sit in your backyard and listen, and read David's book.

PART III:

Flora and Habitat

Green Seduction

Some people fall prey to the dark side. Me, I fell prey to the green side, long ago when I was seduced by plants. One of my earliest memories of Seattle is when my family moved into our new house and I got to choose my bedroom. I picked the one that had a vine growing through the window. I have no clue what the vine was and no recollection of the vine ever entering the window again, but I do know that the bedroom served me well during the many years I lived in it.

Another distant recollection from that time is when I saw a cactus in bloom at the Volunteer Park Conservatory. What a weird plant and flower for a young boy in the Pacific Northwest to see. Is that part of what drew me to the desert southwest many years later?

When I did eventually move to Moab, geology consumed my attention, but over the years I became more and more enchanted with the flora. I took delight in seeing the first green leaves and first flower of spring; discovering the tenacity of life in hanging gardens and pygmy forests; learning new names, such as bastard toadflax, puccoon, and false mockorange (which should be an orange with that double-negative construction, but sadly isn't); and watching cacti bloom in their native habitat. (I still delight in seeing cactus plants blooming.)

Encouraged by the many times I succumbed to greenery, I allowed myself once again to be seduced by a plant when my wife and I were shopping for a house in Seattle. Like most people, we made the home tour scene, seeing the good, the bad, and the truly ugly. Who would want an all-black (fixtures too) bathroom? Then, one day, our agent sent us to a neighborhood well outside of my youthful experiences. Plain from the outside with a grass front yard, a lone crabapple, and three sad-looking rhododendrons, the house was equally as unadorned inside, with renter's-white walls and tan carpets. But the backyard was beyond compare: three magnificent Douglas-firs, the biggest of which we couldn't wrap our arms around. Six weeks later we moved in and have never regretted it. In addition to the three original trees, a now sixty-foot-tall Doug-fir decided to grow in the front yard.

My reminiscences of my past floral seductions were prompted by rereading David Rains Wallace's *The Klamath Knot*. I first read the book in college when it came out—there's even a piece of paper in my book with notes from what looks like my Introduction to Geology course. Wallace's book is a splendid homage to place, exploring plants and animals, geology, and evolution, and still interesting forty years after my initial encounter.

Late in the book, Wallace compares plants and animals in regard to evolution. After noting that his copy of the *Fossils* Golden Nature Guide—those classic pocket-sized nature guides that cover everything from bats to zoo animals—gives short shrift to information about plants, he writes, "In a truly progressive view of evolution, however, plants would be given the greater emphasis because they are the leaders. They always adapt to new climates, new soils, new terrain before animals do."

What further makes Wallace's observation fascinating is that plants are planetary newcomers, only moving onto land about four hundred million years ago, which means they have been doing their thing only for the last

10 percent of Earth's history. But what a thing they have been doing. Plants enabled the development of soils, reduced atmospheric CO_2, and increased O_2, ultimately creating the planetary atmosphere we have evolved to know and love.

I hadn't thought of plants that way, as the colonizers that create, and created, the paths for animals to follow, but I should have as I have regularly seen this in our yard and around Seattle. Wherever there are plants, animals abound, whether they are the many critters I have encountered in our big, backyard Dougs; beavers in the city's many parks; or stumps riddled with woodpeckers holes. And I have seen many locations, such as the "soft estate" ecosystems (as the roadside areas are called in the United Kingdom) along highways, building ledges dotted with plants, or rooftops overtaken by mosses, where plants are exploiting new niches that will attract new animals.

Not only are plants seducers and colonizers, but they are also a gateway. They provide one of the easiest ways for city dwellers to interact with the natural world. Wildflowers, shrubs, and trees and their verdurous partners are always around us, whether in our homes, our yards, or public parks, allowing us to see how they live and die, how animals interact with them, and how they affect our moods. I cannot count the number of times that I have gone into our backyard or simply strolled our neighborhood and been comforted by the vegetation or entranced by the animals making use of the floral habitat. Wow, they are almost as cool as rocks!

Superbloom, Seattle Style

In 2023, epic atmospheric rivers of moisture bathed California and produced stunning superblooms in the desert while we in the Pacific Northwest had an arid spring, at least in terms of what Seattleites are used to experiencing. As of late April, my fair city was about 4.5 inches below our normal precipitation, but thankfully that did not stop one of my favorite wildflowers from creating very localized fields of beauty. If you want your own private superbloom far from floral fanatics, head to seeps and other wet spots, the home of the skunk cabbage.

The great Carl Linnaeus was the first to provide a scientific name for skunk cabbage (albeit one native to Japan and the Kamchatka Peninsula). He named it *Dracontium foliis lanceolatis*, or roughly "little lance-leaved dragon," if my Latin still serves me. Our species is now known as *Lysichiton americanus*, a reference to the spathe, or large yellow bract, that surrounds the flower spike. Shaped like a chiton (a tunic worn by ancient Greeks and Romans), the spathe flares bright before withering and fading, a facet of life noted by the use of the Greek root *lysi-*, meaning "loosen" or "dissolve." The common name references the strong aroma, likened to carrion or feces, which attracts beetle and fly pollinators. Another popular name highlights the spathe: swamp lantern.

Henry David Thoreau was an early observer and commenter on skunk cabbage (the eastern species, *Symplocarpus foetidus*). In his journal, he wrote, "If you are afflicted with melancholy at this season, go to the swamp and see the brave spears of skunk-cabbage buds already advanced toward a new year. Their gravestones are not bespoken yet. Is it the winter of their discontent? Do they seem to have lain down to die, despairing of skunk-cabbagedom? 'Up and at 'em,' 'Give it to 'em,' 'Excelsior,' 'Put it through,'—these are their mottoes."

"Despairing of skunk-cabbagedom" creates such an eminently fine image, but what's curious about Mr. Thoreau's observations is when he made them, on October 31, 1857. His focus was on the autumnal fortitude of the plants, which can poke up their spathe tips in October and November; a botanist friend told me that "probably a small percentage do as a form of bet, hedging if winter is mild."

As Thoreau often did, he illuminated an aspect of nature that others miss, but I think that for many people, myself included, the skunk cabbage's appearance early in the year is a key harbinger of spring. I always look forward to them rising in wet spots, their yolk-yellow brilliance so in contrast to the muted colors of winter. They are a wetland's joyous shout, quick and crystalline, of renewal and rebirth, that the essential destiny of verdurous life will once again return.

One reason skunk cabbage can appear so early, and relatively alone as a fleshy plant, is the calcium oxalate crystals in their leaves and bracts, which prevents predators from consuming the young growth. Needlelike, the crystals cause whoever eats the plants "to suffer transcendent pain," wrote Arthur

Lee Jacobson in *Wild Plants of Greater Seattle*. (I am pretty sure that Arthur Lee has eaten or attempted to eat more native plants than anyone else in Seattle.) Calcium oxalate is also found in many foods, including spinach, rhubarb, and Swiss chard, as well as in kidney stones.

Although the spathe fades away, the leaves persist, emerald dragon tails that can be five feet long. In this land of unrivaled vegetal exuberance, these brilliant shocks of green still draw attention and give the landscape a surprising tropical appearance. April is the time to celebrate the golden glow of the spathe, but your time is limited, as they will soon fade away, a sure sign that summer is on its way.

The Memory of a Tree

To the Indigenous people of the Pacific Northwest, western redcedar has long been the tree of life. Ropes, cradles, and canoes. Homes, hats, baskets, and masks. Bowls and diapers. No object was too commonplace or too grand to be made from these beautiful trees. Their cultural relevance still holds power, and as recently as July 2023, one particular western redcedar became the center of an uproar. The double-trunked tree grows in the Wedgwood neighborhood of northeast Seattle and was slated to be cut down so that new homes could be built on the lot, which led to a vociferous campaign to protect the trees.

With my backyard being home to three massive Douglas-firs, I understand the passion one can develop for trees. They are more than simply beautiful specimens of nature, harbors of habitat, and critically important in creating cleaner and healthier air; they are also beacons of memory, withstanding and witnessing the many changes in their community.

Western redcedars can live for up to 1,500 years, so the Wedgwood one is probably just a youngster. Given its size, let's say that the cedar is 150 years old. Consider what has transpired in the tree's life. In its youth, the tree's terminal growth stem was cut or broken, which caused two new stems to grow into the present double trunk. Cutting the tree down would erase the memory of who clipped the stem (maybe a hungry deer) or of the event that broke it (possibly Seattle's biggest snowstorm, a massive 1916 dumper of more than three feet).

The Wedgwood cedar is old enough that when it began to grow, our very atmosphere was vastly different. The amount of carbon dioxide was about 288 parts per million, and the planet was emerging from the Little Ice Age. By the time the tree was sixty, the CO_2 level was still around 300 parts per million, but then in the 1960s the level began to rise steeply and consistently: 320 to 350 to 390 to its present 420. Few other local forms of life (one being geoducks) beyond a tree such as this cedar bear testimony to that preindustrial era, when the air was sweet and clean.

At the beginning of the Wedgwood cedar's life, the tree was surrounded by forest, most likely other western redcedars, along with western hemlocks and Douglas-firs. Cedars often prefer slightly wetter spots than hemlock and fir, so the little sprout could have started near a long-lost seep, a location that could have attracted generations of wildlife who could have made a home in the cedar. Over its lifetime, the tree has been visited by countless animals and shared its space with wildflowers, fungi, shrubs, bacteria, and other trees. It has been a home, a refuge, and more recently, a link to the past.

When we cut down a tree, we sever many links that have helped bind together this place we call Seattle. We also erase a memory of the Native people who have inhabited this landscape since time immemorial. Just north of the cedar at Thornton Creek was a fishing weir where people could have harvested salmon. Did they walk by this tree? A precontact trail (now long gone) ran between Lake Washington and a bog (called Slo'q`qed in Lushootseed) at what is now Northgate Station, so the first residents must have traveled nearby. In addition, the Wedgwood cedar is a culturally modified tree, according to Jaime Martin of the Snoqualmie Tribe. Traditionally, modifications might include bending a branch as a directional signpost or

WEDGWOOD

Developer Albert Balch named the neighborhood for the famed English pottery because his wife, Edith, liked the craftsmanship and distinctive blue color. Other curious Seattle neighborhood names include Magnolia, named in 1856 by Lieutenant George Davidson of the US Coast Survey because he mistook madrone trees for magnolias; Laurelhurst, named for madrones, which some have called laurels; and Delridge, originally called Dell Ridge but shortened by government fiat in 1940.

stripping part of the bark for cultural uses, each an important cultural connection preserved in the memory of the cedar.

More recently, the Wedgwood cedar has witnessed newer arrivals. One was a fellow member of my book club. In 1957, Stan and Marion Gartler built a house a few blocks from the Wedgwood cedar. Stan worked at the University of Washington and did seminal research in somatic cell genetics. Lives such as Stan's and Marion's have taken place all around the Wedgwood cedar, and its loss would have eliminated the imprints of those generations of families found within the cells of the tree.

For some reason, the Wedgwood cedar survived over the decades as its neighbors succumbed to development. Its legacy is a true treasure, a testimony to change and luck and serendipity—and to memory. By protecting trees such as the Wedgwood cedar, we preserve not only a beautiful and valuable part of the community but also the stories of place and the memories that help bring us together.

Postscript: Thanks to the tireless efforts of the Snoqualmie Indian Tribe and citizen activists, as of 2024 the tree was saved and still grows.

Tails of the City: Cattail

I have long been a fan of short skinnies—that is, the relatively low-growing, stalky plants that pop up periodically about Seattle. Two of my favorite bear the appropriate word *tail* in their names, a fine indicator of their narrow nature. More appreciated is the cattail, *Typha latifolia*, described by the great naturalist and forager Euell Gibbons as the "supermarket of the swamps." (Mr. G was once well-known for promoting Grape-Nuts—my favorite cereal—and, by the way, lived in Seattle in the 1930s.) In contrast, horsetails (*Equisetum arvense*) led none other than one of Seattle's most famous plant guys, Ciscoe Morris, to label them as "the worst weed you can get in your garden."

Cattail deserves its reputation as a long-appreciated plant. Ethnobotanist Nancy Turner has written that it was "probably the most important basket and mat weaving material," for local Indigenous people noting that it was used for bags, baskets, canoe sails, clothing, cradles, mats, nets, and twine. The cottony down made it into pillows, mattresses, and diapers. People ate the leaves, spike, and rootstock; tattooed with cattail charcoal; and incorporated the down into a variety of burial and mortuary rituals. A 2001 paper in the *Journal of Ethnobiology* notes that "the underlying theme linking cattail down and concepts of death, the afterworld and spiritual cleansing may be the symbolic potency of the colour white."

By the way, not everyone likes the spelling *cattail*. The British, in particular, favor *cat's-tail*; I am okay with that, considering it dates back to 1548, when one William Turner wrote of "cattes tayle," or "Reedmace," as some preferred. He also added, "It hath a black thinge Almost at the head of the stalk lyke black velvuet." In addition, some people refer to cattails as bulrush, a name more appropriate for sedges in the genus *Schoenoplectus* (formerly *Scirpus*), which includes plants known as tule, another plant widely used by Indigenous people. My favorite name, "the Asparagus of the Cossacks," comes from the 1850 *Annals of Horticulture*, which states, "It may be cut, stewed, prepared for serving with yolk of eggs, enhancing the flavour with nutmeg and salt."

SLO'Q`QED

A Lushootseed word meaning "bald head," it references the relatively treeless nature of a former bog, now the location of the Northgate Station shopping complex. Like most Native place- and animal names, this one is no longer in common parlance, but several words still persist. *Geoduck* comes from the Lushootseed gwidəq, meaning "dig deep." The name of Licton Springs (a small natural spring in north Seattle) is a corruption of the Lushootseed liq'ted, which means "red" or "paint," and Shilshole, the location of a Native village site, comes from sHulsHóól, meaning "tucked away inside."

What got me thinking about cattails is how often I notice them on the side of I-5. Even when there is no traffic and I am traveling sixty miles per hour, I can easily see what look like tall brown hot dogs on a stick but are actually long green leaves and stems topped by spikes of tightly packed flowers. I have no idea how common these cattail communities are along I-5, but they seem surprisingly widespread. Those who study the spike tell us that they (the spike, not the researchers) are normally six times as long as they are thick and that female flowers grow below the males. When pollinated, cattails produce white cottony down, which many people like to produce by squeezing the spike, if you know what I mean.

Plants spread either via their copious seeds or rhizomes and are a pioneer species that colonizes and does well on disturbed habitat. This is probably why I see the little ecosystems along the interstate; the plants are taking advantage of areas that collect runoff and form micro-wetlands, an ironic development, considering roads have long displaced wetlands.

Wetlands are incredibly important to the overall community health of the flora, fauna, air, and water. Unfortunately, far too many people view them as problematic waste sites, and many of Seattle's wetlands have been paved over or destroyed. For example, six bogs once enhanced the city with their floating mats of sphagnum, pink-blossomed bog laurel, white-flowered Labrador tea, cranberry, and sundew, a carnivorous plant. All are gone, including two replaced by shopping malls: Northgate Station and University Village. And, when Lake Washington was lowered by nine feet for the canal and locks, more than a thousand acres of wetlands dried up, including the areas of Renton Municipal Airport, Boeing's Renton Factory, Stan Sayres Memorial Park, and Genesee Park. But there's good news: years of restoration has returned one of the drained areas around the Center for Urban Horticulture back to more wetland-like habitat, visited by more than two hundred bird species.

In case you think that wetland destruction is a thing of the past, in August 2021, the US government had to weaken wetlands protection because of a horrible, pro-business US Supreme Court ruling (*Sackett v. Environmental Protection Agency*, No. 21-454). When will we learn to take the long view and recognize the important contributions of wetlands to ecosystem health over short-term profits?

Tails of the City: Horsetail

Now, let's turn to a less favored plant, at least in the horticultural community: horsetails (*Equisetum arvense*). (It wasn't until I started writing this essay that I made the connection between *Equus*, the genus for horses, and *Equisetum*, the genus of horsetails. Funny how the brain works, or doesn't.) Notorious, and apparently reviled, for their promiscuous and rampant growth, our local horsetails are one- to two-foot-tall fingers of hollow green stems sporting a plume of wiry, several-inch-long branches. I have a good friend who will remain nameless because I don't want to embarrass her, but she loves to pull apart the branches section by section because they make such a "satisfying break," or so she claims regarding her curious passion for delimbing innocent plants. One can do the same with the stems, which make an audible pop when separated.

Like cattails, horsetails (*E. arvense* and other species in the genus) have long been culturally important in the region. In Erna Gunther's *Ethnobotany of Western Washington*, she writes of Klallam, Makah, Quileute, and Quinault people eating the young stems, often one of the first green shoots to sprout in spring, as well as eating the little bulbs on the root stock, cooking and mixing them with whale or seal oil. Swinomish informants also told

Gunther of using the plants with dogfish skin as sandpaper, as well as to polish arrow shafts.

Read up on horsetails and you generally come across two statements such as these: horsetails have been around since the time of the dinosaurs, and horsetails were ginormous and towered taller than a nine-story building. The first statement is correct, as *Equisetum* species were around during the era of dinosaurs, having evolved around the same time as the big beasts, in the Triassic. According to Andres Elgorriaga, one of the leading researchers on *Equisetum* evolution, it is one of the oldest, if not the oldest, genera of vascular plants on Earth. What makes them particularly stunning, Andres told me, is that the genus *Equisetum* has changed relatively little since their initial evolution and still possess an extensive rhizome system; hollow, aerial stems with minute leaves fused, forming a sheath; "jointed" non-woody stems with a telescopic type of growth; and terminal reproductive structures named "strobilus."

But *Equisetum* species weren't terribly tall. Back in the Carboniferous (359 to 298 million years ago and named because of the coal deposits from this period), when there was more atmospheric oxygen than in our modern world (except during the 1990s heyday of oxygen bars), some horsetails were the trees of the day and would have dwarfed all dinosaurs. They were not, however, *Equisetum* but *Calamites*, a close cousin in a different family. I know I'm splitting horsehairs, but what do you expect from me?

Another long-popular, but incorrect, attribution about *Equisetum* is the plant's ability to accumulate gold in their stems. In the late 1930s, Slovakian researchers reported gold concentrations in *Equisetum* between 3,500 and 6,100 times the plant's substrate. Ever since, scientists, naturalists, and prospectors have perpetuated the idea that there's gold in them thar horsetails. A 1981 report noted that horsetails grow on auriferous mine tailings and

are often the only species present, but the authors concluded that *Equisetum* actually indicated arsenic, so like many a claim about gold, it's useless. *Equisetum* species do, however, accumulate silica, which gives them another common name, scouring rush, though I hope you know that they are not a rush at all. They are effective scrubbers, though.

Like cattails, horsetails prefer moist soil and are generally found growing near seeps. At least, that's where I think of seeing them in the Seattle area. Many people, however, think of *Equisetum* as a yard miscreant, a plant that takes over their well-tended garden space, bullies out their preferred plants, and becomes a floral menace. I appreciate that concern, but when I see *Equisetum*, I can't help but rejoice, thinking that these plants have persisted for hundreds of millions of years doing what they do. Why should we be so dismissive, disrespectful, and downright nasty to them? In the long run, what we do will not make much of a difference; *Equisetum* have faced far worse than us, having survived the biggest mass extinction ever on Earth, two hundred million years ago, as well as the one that killed off the nonavian dinosaurs, sixty-six million years ago. I am sure that *Equisetum* will be here long after the last gardener.

The Devils' Club

Few plants are as prickly as devil's club or as valued by the people of this region. Armed with spines nearly anywhere you or a hungry animal might touch the plant, devil's club is one of the more formidable and intimidating plants of the understory. (Just to be clear, in the botanical world, prickles, spines, and thorns are different. As my friend Sarah Gage wrote in a fine column for the Washington Native Plant Society blog, "Broadly speaking, spines derive from leaves, prickles from epidermis, and thorns from stems." So, there you have it, and now I am going to ignore the definition and mix the terms.)

The plants also have lovely flowers and bright red berries, eaten by birds and relished by bears. One study in Alaska found that black and brown bears collectively can consume more than 100,000 devil's club berries per hour. And, since we all know the answer to the eternal question about what bears do in the woods, these meals end up spreading more than 518,000 seeds per square mile every hour, which are then further dispersed by "scatter-hoarding small mammals." The study's authors concluded that bears were uniquely important in the distribution of devil's club. Botanists refer to this fecal-based system of seed dispersal as endozoochory. I, of course, encourage you to try to drop this word into a conversation whenever you can.

Bears, sadly, are not responsible for the distribution of devil's club in Seattle. As you might suspect with me and my interests, geology bears that responsibility. (One of the pleasures of English is being able to use *bears* twice when the words have absolutely no etymological connection.) The plants prefer moist areas, such as the many glacially formed seeps that dot the city, often in ravines.

Despite the prickly spines—or because of them—devil's club has long been used by Indigenous people. Ethnobotanist Nancy Turner has described

dozens of traditional uses that addressed the physical and spiritual realms of medicine, as well as uses for fishing and as a pigment. Swallowed, chewed, or rubbed onto the body, devil's club infusions and decoctions have been used for pain relief, arthritis, diabetes, stomachaches, skin disorders, colds, and fevers, to name a few of the dozens of treated ailments. It could also aid in gambling, protect against witchcraft, work as a love charm, and provide luck in hunting. Few plants were and are as valued.

Turner also found that almost every Native language had its own distinct name for the plant. The translated names include big thorn, bear's berries, codfish lure plant, prickle-big, and gambling sticks.

The first non-Native known to collect the plant was the inestimable Archibald Menzies, who obtained specimens at Nootka Sound on Vancouver Island in 1787 or 1788. His specimens were labeled as *Aralia erinacea*, an indication of the plant's inclusion in the same family (Araliaceae) as ginseng. They have also been designated as *Fatsia horridus* (a derivation of the Japanese word for the number eight, in reference to the leaves' eight lobes) and *Panax horridum* but are now known as *Oplopanax horridus*.

As with many plants, the common and scientific names tell as much about what the namers thought of the plant as the plant itself. The common name (another one was devil's walking stick) appears to have been first used in the 1870s, often accompanied by such qualifiers as *vile plant, most offensive plant*, and *hateful thing*, and supplemented with complaints about getting pricked by the spines. The scientific name is a curious mix. *Oplo* is from the Greek for "weapon" or "shield." *Panax* is also of Greek origin, meaning "all healing," such as in *panacea*. Thus, we have a horrible, all-healing weapon, which I guess could also be read as a horrible shield against healing, though that'd be completely wrong. No wonder I like names and their origins.

Apparently, the devil, or those who appropriated his moniker, got around. There are hundreds of places named for the prince of darkness, from the Big Devil Bayou in Texas to the Devils Washbasin in the Goat Rocks Wilderness (at least we know that some people thought the big baddie was concerned with cleanliness). I assume that many are quite beautiful and enchanting places, so why do they merit a reference to Beelzebub? It seems that if you didn't like the guy (or whatever or whoever it is), you'd want to avoid honoring him by placing his name permanently on a location, but place-names have often been used as honorifics for no good reason.

The Joys of Repeat Travel

When I worked as a park ranger at Arches National Park, a common line I heard from visitors was "Oh, I've already hiked that trail. What's another one I can do?" Although I have asked a similar question, probably too many times, I was also troubled by it. Yes, we may have hiked a particular trail already, but what did we see and what did we miss on our single encounter? How much more would we have observed by walking the trail again? How would it differ in summer versus spring, on a rainy day instead of sunny one, or at night, when few of us venture out?

Over the past several years, I have had the good fortune to go on an almost weekly handcycle (a low-to-the-ground tricycle powered by the rider's arms) ride on the Centennial Trail near Arlington, forty miles north of Seattle. The ride itself is nothing spectacular. My pal Scott and I cross over a river and a creek, pass through open fields and second-growth forest, pedal along a busy road, and hit trail's end about 7.5 miles north at the historic Nakashima barn. What makes it an enjoyable ride to me are the accumulated observations from riding it well over a hundred times.

NAKASHIMA BARN

Located at the north end of the Centennial Trail, the property began to be farmed by the Nakashima family around 1910. Anti-Japanese laws, however, prevented them from acquiring the land until 1937. Then, in 1942, the family was incarcerated in California and Idaho under Executive Order 9066, which forced 120,000 West Coast Japanese Americans into internment camps. The Nakashima family never returned to the property, one more World War II story of this country's disgraceful treatment of Japanese Americans.

One day we saw an immature black bear walking down the trail. We knew bears trod the trail because we'd seen—and tried to avoid, though it's harder to do with three wheels—their scat (dark and seedy, sometimes turdiform, sometimes splatty), but this was the first time we encountered a defecator in person. We were quite pleased that we did not see the young bear's mother; we suspected she may have been nearby. Other fellow mammals we have seen include coyotes, foxes, deer, a weasel, rabbits, squirrels, horses, and dogs (ranging from ones in strollers to one that seemingly wants to kill us every time we ride by).

We have also been blessed by sounds. Along the wetlands in spring we hear male Pacific chorus frogs advertising their virility and male Song Sparrows incessantly chittering about their territory. The spiraling melody of Swainson's Thrushes regularly resounds on our ride, along with the catlike mew call of Spotted Towhees and the high chirping of Dark-eyed Juncos. Bald Eagles, Red-tailed Hawks, and Cooper's Hawks regularly let us—or more likely another animal—know via their calls that they are nearby, as

do Northern Flickers and Downy Woodpeckers pounding trees in search of insects.

Because we sit so low on our handcycles, we have a special opportunity to notice the ground and what covers it. In addition to the aforementioned bear poop, we have ridden by coyote, horse, dog, and deer feces; garter snakes (only seen on sunny days exploiting the warm pavement); quite a few voles and moles (always dead); and approximately a gazillion slugs. Seasonal trail users, slugs tend to appear in early spring and disappear when dry and warmer weather arrives.

As the weather changes, so does the nonliving ground cover. In autumn, yellow to brown leaves quiet the sound of our tires on concrete. Winter brings storm-broken branches and twigs, the rare snowfall, and one time, the even rarer hair ice. With spring, skunk cabbage explodes in the wetlands, alder catkins litter our route, and cottonwoods release a storm of cotton that can accumulate so densely on the trail that it appears we are riding on snow. In summer, cut grass borders the trail, easily the most unpleasant seasonal feature, as our low profile allows the grass and grit to get in our hair and mouths, down our shirts, and everywhere.

We always slow down as we pass over the confluence of the north and south forks of the Stillaguamish River, wondering which will carry more water. We have seen flow rates from less than one thousand cubic feet per second to more than sixty thousand cubic feet per second. In summer, when the river is low, the water is a clear greenish blue, and we can see the gravelly bottom. After a rain, the water turns muddy brown and carries debris that accumulates in a massive logjam, big enough that plants have started to grow on it. Despite the many times we have crossed the river, I still enjoy the anticipation of seeing the ever-changing patterns of eddies, whirlpools, and vortices as the two forks meet, mingle, and mate. And, in the autumn of

2023, when we walked instead of rode for several weeks, we saw hundreds of migrating Chinook salmon, truly a beautiful and hopeful sight.

If we had ridden this trail only once or twice, I would have missed this incredible diversity of sight, sound, and smell, and the trail might have seemed boring and lacking in interest. Riding this route regularly over the years, though, has opened my senses to the trail's complexity and beauty. While I have come to know the sections that always trouble me and where I can coast and enjoy the speed, and I have started to get a feel for the seasonal changes, I am still surprised and pleased by what we see, how it constantly varies, and how I continue to discover new aspects of the nature of the place.

Four Seasons

I always look forward to the cooling days of fall, to being able to wear a different set of clothes (always important for a man of my sartorial splendor), and to the beautiful colors that saturate our trees. But I am no bigger fan of fall than I am of any of the other seasons, though I am a bit partial to spring, and feel that all our seasons have their merits and detractions.

Curiously, or so I think, I have a good friend who argues that Seattle does not have four seasons. She bases her reasoning on her upbringing in Iowa and its distinct seasonality. In winter, she was unpleasantly cold; in summer, unpleasantly hot and humid; and then she had spring and fall. To her, Seattle's lack of too hot and too cold means that our fair city has only way-too-long spring and fall.

I strongly disagree. Our seasons may not be as distinct as my pal's childhood seasons—which, even she admitted, could be defined as miserable, spring, miserable, and autumn—but you can distinguish ours.

Winter: Short days, in the pre-Covid era, when my wife worked away from home, she disappeared to and returned from work in darkness. Gray days, when the light of the sky and air blend together and the world seems flatter. Sunny days, when light cuts through the leafless trees in our yard and illuminates our house—and highlights where we haven't dusted. Aurally

SUNBREAK

A splendid turn of word for a place like Seattle, where clouds can block the sun for weeks at a time, *sunbreak* first appeared in 1826 in the book-length poem *Dartmoor*, written by Noel Thomas Carrington. "The few bright sunbreaks, that have cheer'd My toilsome pilgrimage!" Carrington wasn't actually referencing true sunbreaks, or bursts of sunshine, but used the term as a metaphor for hope and uplift, certainly still true to today's residents of Seattle, who rely on these moments of light in the dark of winter. Another fine but seldom-used term is *filtered sunshine*, incorporated into a 1924 Chamber of Commerce pamphlet as "best for all, and vital to the development of the most energetic peoples."

pleasant mornings, when the whiny call of Bald Eagles from nearby trees prompts me to arise. Too-cold fingers and toes on my weekly handcycle ride. The occasional snowfall dampening sound yet also opening up the ecosystem by revealing the tracks of animals that I don't see without the amanuensis of snow. Hot chocolate and popcorn, our favorite revival foods after a long urban walk. Winter is also about the night sky and two of my favorite constellations, the Pleiades (a.k.a. the Seven Sisters, or Subaru in Japanese) and Orion, the great hunter of the night.

Spring: Tempestuous weather and chances of snow, rain, fog, mizzle, drizzle, and sunbreaks make life more stimulating and lead to more decisions about what to wear while walking, hiking, and biking. Color returns as flowers begin to pop open, bringing the buzzing of early pollinators. Singing returns with birds announcing their fertility potential. New shades of green appear in what looks like internal lighting of incipient foliage. Of course, we further benefit by having relatively mild weather (low temperatures and copious rain) in our winters, which contributes to the luscious growth of our conifers. Spring is also a time when south-migrating Canada geese ink the sky with their V-line skeins, a sure sign that change is afoot, or on-wing, in this situation.

Summer: Hot days prompt plants to sprout and grow and thrive, and our house disappears from the street, hidden by the small forest in the front yard. Long days coax me to get up very early to run or bike and go to sleep with light still in the sky. Brown lawns force me to wonder again at the perverse nature of our climate that the grass goes dormant and dismal at the time of year when people most often like to be on it (and, in my mind, waste water on it). Melting snow reveals cragged mountain peaks, and the rim of white that surrounds us morphs to the greens and grays of forest and rocky summits. Summer also means local produce and relishing mountain huckleberries and blueberries, flavorful tomatoes, basketball-sized

heads of lettuce, our yard's golden raspberries, and peas so sweet they could be labeled candy.

Fall: Brisk temperatures and my stylish mien lead to much rejoicing from all who encounter me! As chlorophyll breaks down with cooler temperatures and shorter days (trees unequivocally recognize seasons), honey-, mustard-, mahogany-, and brick-colored leaves begin to bless the region with warm hues. The drying leaves result in some of my favorite fall sounds—crunch, crackle, and rasp—when I bike through the accumulations of foliage on streets. Fall also is the time of spiders, or at least, that's when many of us notice them, particularly orb weavers and giant house spiders, the former of which build beautiful and intricate webs that often dance in the light of a dewy morn.

Smoke: Sadly, we seem to have acquired a fifth season, when fires dirty the air, cause itchy throats and eyes, and produce tomato sunsets. I don't think Iowa can make this claim.

With the exception of our newest season, I always look forward to the seasonal change. Each is a time of renewal as the natural world adapts to the new temperatures, changes in the amount of daylight, and the migration of animals. With each new season comes a grace note enticing me outside, a herald of new opportunities, and a gift that I can celebrate again and again.

Hair Ice

One of my joys of discovery is heading down an absorbing path of seeking out more information in newspapers and scientific journals, reaching out to friends and colleagues, or delving into the books waiting to be probed on my bookshelf. No matter where these paths lead me, I feel I am rewarded by the knowledge I gain and the connections I make.

The most recent time this happened was on a very cold morning when my wife and I were walking with a pal of ours at Tolt River–John MacDonald Park. The air was brisk, the ground frosty, and the decaying tree limbs erupting in beauty. In particular, we were attracted by a curious phenomenon none of us had ever seen. Sprouting out of the downed wood were what looked like tufts of fine hair, brilliantly white and curled like Albert Einstein's mane but better kempt.

Known appropriately as hair ice, this fragile and ephemeral feature owes its origin to the winter-active fungus *Exidiopsis effusa*. It is a white root fungus (please feel free to use this as the name of your next rock band) capable of decomposing the lignin—a complex organic polymer—that gives wood its strength, something very few organisms can accomplish. In his thoughtful book *Entangled Life*, Merlin Sheldrake writes that the decomposition is accomplished by "highly reactive molecules, known as 'free radicals,' which

crack open lignin . . . [via] 'enzymatic combustion.'" It's probably less dangerous than it sounds.

But back to what *E. effusa* did along the river. The fungus helped create the tufts of hair ice via a process called ice segregation. After the initial formation of ice nuclei in the limb, new ice extracts additional water from the wood, which leads to more ice growth that eventually extrudes out through holes in the limb's surface. If no *E. effusa* is present, the ice turns crusty, but if *E. effusa* is present, it provides decomposed lignin and tannin that act as a combination curler and hair spray, shaping and setting the fine strands of ice growing out of the wood. Each strand is 0.0008 inch wide and up to 8 inches long; for comparison, human hair ranges from 0.002 to 0.005 inches wide.

Part of what makes the science so splendid to me is that the first person to propose the fungus and hair ice connection was one of my heroes, Alfred Wegener, in 1918. A meteorologist, explorer, and hot-air balloon experimenter, Wegener is best known for his theory of continental drift, which proposed that Earth's land masses had once formed a single great continent. Like his theory on hair ice, decades would pass before scientists later proved he was correct.

We in the Puget lowland are lucky because hair ice grows only within a limited band between 45 degrees and 55 degrees north latitude. It can be found on the downed limbs of broad-leafed trees, including two of our resident species, red alder and bigleaf maple.

Wandering the trails, we kept stopping to marvel over the strands of shimmering evanescence. When we touched them, we found that the hair ice had a curious density of texture that I now wonder may have been the product of the decomposed lignin, as if their structural strength had been transferred from the wood to ice, as if all were part of one amazing, interwoven community. Walking along, I felt that each limb covered in hair ice was a beautiful reward for being part of this community.

The Vicissitudes of Nanohabitat

One winter day when it was snowing, my wife and I took a short walk from our house. We headed north two blocks, then east over I-5, and up a slight ridge. In doing so, we passed through a phase-changing temperature gradient. At our house, the snow was not sticking to the sidewalk. At the apex of the ridge, the snow stuck. Total elevation change was about one hundred feet.

Depending on which website one trusts, with every one thousand feet in elevation we could have risen, we would have lost between 3.5 and 5.5 degrees Fahrenheit. Since we ascended only one hundred feet, the temperature only dropped between about a third and half of a degree, but still just enough of a nanohabitat change to allow snow to remain on pavement.

Several years ago, I also passed through a similar temperature gradient in a downtown building. I had ridden up to the forty-seventh floor of the Seattle Municipal Tower and done a bit of research. When I looked out a nearby window, it was snowing, but when I got down to the ground floor, it was raining. Dropping more than 470 feet, I had gone from snowy cold air to rainy warm air, what you might call urban snow virga (rain

CONVERGENCE ZONE

The term first appeared in print in 1969 in an unpublished internal National Weather Service document but did not become popular until the 1980s. It describes how weather from the Pacific coast splits in two around the Olympic Mountains. One wave of air flows down the Strait of Juan de Fuca and one through the Chehalis Gap, a glacial outwash–carved lowland between the Olympics to the north and the Willapa Hills to the south. The uniting of the twained fronts, which often occurs around Everett, results in increased precipitation, both liquid and solid. Depending on the weather circumstances, the convergence zone can move up and down the Sound.

that evaporates before reaching the ground), or snirga, if I may coin a portmanteau.

The subtle variation my wife and I experienced on our walk is one of the challenges in snow forecasting in Seattle. When it snows here, it generally happens right around the freezing point. Combine the mutability of topographic temperatures with our big bodies of water (Lake Washington and Puget Sound), which hold heat longer than pavement, and it's very challenging to provide a definitive snow accumulation forecast for the entire city. So be nice to forecasters; they're people too.

But, of course, there's even more complexity. On our walk, snow accumulated in a hodgepodge of patterns. (By the way, Geoffrey Chaucer helped popularize the related *hotch-potch*, which came from *hotch-pot*, or a stew with varied ingredients.) The most obvious was the difference in accumulation on grass versus pavement, primarily because grass retains less heat than a sidewalk and provides a cooler surface where snow can collect. More beautiful was how leaves looked like snow whisperers, as if they had charmed the snow to land only on them. This would be a novel phenomenon but, alas, has to do with the leaves also providing a cooler surface than the pavement.

Shrubs and trees also play a part. Not surprisingly, less snow accumulated under leafy and well-needled vegetation, but the same happened with bare trees. I wonder if, in addition to capturing the snow, the branches changed the flow of air enough to alter accumulation. Considering the 16 percent I got on the physics quiz in college, you probably shouldn't trust any ideas I write that have anything to do with physics.

Proximity to walls also influenced where snow remained. Solar radiation bouncing off south-facing walls added enough warmth to sidewalks to keep

them bare. There were also many areas with no discernible reason for where snow wasn't. Were there sewer pipes with warm water heating pavement, geothermal deposits, or not very good snow sweepers?

So, what does all this mean? Some climate change skeptics say that we don't need to worry about one or two degrees of temperature increase. They are wrong. As I witnessed with the minimal temperature variation I experienced, little is required to alter what happens with snow. In addition, what I saw is predicted to play out in our regional precipitation patterns: climate change–induced warming will mean that the mountains of the Pacific Northwest should get less snow and more rain. Precipitation is expected to increase, but because of warming temperatures, snow will arrive later in autumn and stop falling earlier in spring. The impacts on salmon, recreation, and urban water supply will be dramatic.

Our planet and our neighborhood are sensitive to temperature change. As I walk the streets around my home, I cannot help but be fascinated by the beautiful effects of small variations and worried about the detrimental effects of the big changes we are inflicting on our planet.

Rain Shadows and Other Ephermalities

As I was walking one autumn day through a light mist along a crowded, tree-lined street in downtown Seattle, I looked down at the sidewalk and noticed a feature I hadn't ever considered: the patterns of sweetgum leaves on the concrete. They had been formed by leaf tannins—the same acid that colors creeks and flavors wines—that rain leached onto the pavement. In plants, tannins aid in defense against herbivores and help regulate nutrient cycling and abiotic stress tolerance. These rain shadows, as I call them, though some people prefer *ghost leaves*, are a wonderful trace of life, an ephemeral sign of a plant or animal.

I have long been interested in such evanescent evidence and the clues they provide to life around me. Subtle and short lived, they are yet another joy of being attentive. Here are some of my favorites, and the terms I coined to describe them.

Flight maps: Fleeting and fluid, the shadows produced by birds flying overhead are always a thrill to encounter. I have seen such flight maps in the city and in the backcountry. I like to think they give me eyes in the back of

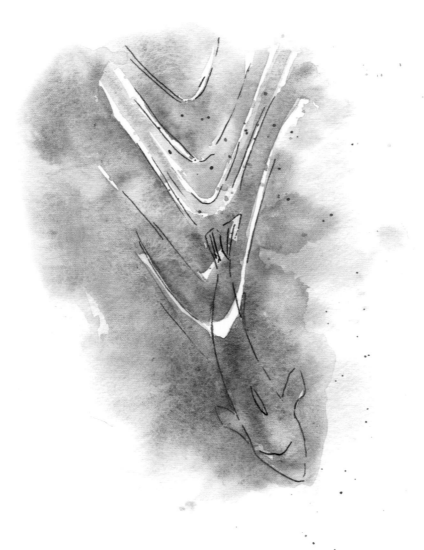

my head as I am alerted to birds flying above or behind me. When I look around and try to figure out who produced the shadow on the ground, I am often rewarded by seeing small birds, such as juncos and robins, or larger ones, including ravens, ducks, and Turkey Vultures. But sometimes I am too late, and the shadow producer has vanished, leaving behind no trace of his or her existence.

Fin trails: Once when I was crossing a bridge over the Pilchuck River on the Centennial Trail with my friend Scott, he pointed out fish below. I didn't see them at first but eventually discerned their V-shaped ripples headed upstream. Formed by the fish's dorsal fins, these fin trails allowed me to track the fish into shallower water, where I could see them clearly. Dozens, many at least two feet long, swam below, following their primal urge to return and spawn in their natal stream. State and tribal biologists told me that we were seeing Chinook salmon (they had counted more than a hundred in the river) and that their numbers were going up because of the removal of a dam upstream.

Mob swoops: My most consistent ephemerality is crows dive-bombing a predator. They usually start ten to fifteen feet above their perceived risk, drop down just above the other bird, and slingshot out of attack range. I have seen crows mob swoop Red-tailed Hawks, Bald Eagles, and Barred Owls, all known to find a good meal in a baby crow, as well as the parents. Better known simply as mobbing, this behavior has a long definition basically to the effect of "Even though you are bigger and badder than my gang, we are still going to harass you just so you know that we know about you and your ilk." Mobbing is often a taught from one generation to the next and between unrelated birds.

Ephemeral, of course, comes from *ephemera,* first used in 1398 to refer to a disease that lasts only a day. Since 1938, though, *ephemera* has been used to refer to "printed matter of no lasting value except to collectors," according to the *Oxford English Dictionary*. Similar to the printed matter, my ecological ephemera may have no lasting value, except to those who care, and for us, of course, they are invaluable.

An Ode to Our Front Yard

There was a splendid story in the *New York Times* in December 2022 titled "They Fought the Lawn. And the Lawn's Done." (I have to applaud the *New York Times* for *sort of* referencing a fine song by the Clash.) The story centered on Janet and Jeff Crouch and their yard, which they planted with shrubs, trees, and annuals that would benefit wildlife. "You're thinking more about the soil, and its inhabitants, and how it fits together in the ecosystem," said Janet. But their neighbor saw otherwise. He couldn't enjoy his own property because of the "mess of a jungle" next door.

In addition, and apparently most annoying of all, the Crouches were "planting shrubs and bushes in no particular order." (Should they have been planted alphabetically, by size, color, shape, speed of growth, or flowering time?) Furthermore, complained the upset neighbor, the out-of-order yard was "attracting rodents, deer, snakes and bats."

My first thought was "Bats!" I am so jealous . . . and inspired. We had recently put up bat boxes in our backyard, trying to entice these astonishing animals to roost. We'd seen them around our house, so I was hopeful.

I can relate to the Crouches, not in having annoying neighbors, but in having a front yard almost completely devoid of grass. When we bought our house in 1998, the front yard was lawn with three rhododendrons (two have died, and the other looks like we have tormented it nigh until death) and a crabapple tree (mostly hidden). Now the yard is a tangle of vegetation so bounteous it hides the house in the summer and creates a tunnel of verdancy between our driveway and the front door.

When we converted the yard to wild, we were like the Crouches, unaware of the correct order to plant. We simply went with native vegetation, including cascara, bleeding heart, salal, Nootka rose, snowberry, camas, wild ginger, and oceanspray. We also planted rosemary, culinary sage, a butterfly bush (since replaced), and a cherry tree, better described as a stick at the time of planting. It is now a huge, cherry-producing tree, though we rarely get any, being outcompeted by more mobile rapscallions such as robins, crows, and

squirrels. (I periodically mess with the squirrels by shooting water at them, which has little effect beyond reaffirming my immaturity.)

As one should expect, other plants have exploited the habitat. These freelancers include swordferns, native blackberry, and a Douglas-fir that is now about twice as tall as our house. Two years ago, we attached a nest box to the tree. Within a day, a Black-capped Chickadee came to inspect it and decided, after further exploration, that it would work for a

CAMAS

Often written as *quamash*, *camas* is derived from the language of the Nez Perce people. The Lewis and Clark Expedition folks were the first Europeans to encounter it. Sergeant John Ordway wrote of the root on September 22, 1805, ". . . which they call Commass. The roots grow in these plains. They have kills [kilns] engeaniously made where they Sweet [sweat] these roots and make them Sweet and good to the taste." In Lushootseed, the flowers are called cabid, though they were also widely known as camas, a term adopted into Chinook Jargon.

home. Since then, chickadees have nested regularly; flickers and juncos have stopped by the box too.

I have previously mentioned the black hawthorn and the annual visit by Cedar Waxwings, but the tree has hosted others. While sitting in our living room one evening, we heard noises clearly not made by humans. When I opened the shade, four raccoons were staring at me. We eyed each other for a few minutes, and then they ignored me. So, I did the same (five can play that game) and shut the shade. Others who take advantage of our front yard ecosystem include the occasional little brown and gray birds (Black-capped Chickadees, Chestnut-backed Chickadees, and Bewick's Wrens), scatterings of flitterers (Bushtits and Golden-crowned and Ruby-crowned Kinglets), dashes of color (Anna's Hummingbirds and Townsend's Warblers), and the ubiquitous and pleasant (robins and juncos). There may also be a hand trowel that we think we left out there and cannot locate.

The green takeover, in particular by the Nootka roses, which, if left to their own devices, would render the yard completely impenetrable, if they didn't lose out to snowberries, also hid an apple tree, which I didn't discover until it was about twenty feet tall. Another time, I found a fifteen-foot-tall maple (non-native). The only downside of our new yard is the lack of sunlight. The lawn's former open space has been reduced to a single, small spot to grow vegetables, and the big trees have shaded the blueberry bushes, which no longer produce because of the lack of sunlight. (The shade also keeps our house cooler in the summer.)

I know we are part of a much larger movement of homeowners who have transformed their yards from grass to wild. I regularly encounter such yards on my walks and runs around town. I am sure that many neighbors of such yards do not rejoice in conversions to wildness, but I am also sure that there are far more plants and animals that appreciate the gesture.

An Ode to Our Backyard

Thanks to the Douglas-firs in our backyard, I have watched Mallards paddle about our flooded flat garage roof under the trees and reveled in the brilliant yellow flashes of Wilson's Warblers. I have wondered about the stories shared between the Brown Creepers ascending the trees and Red-breasted Nuthatches descending them. I have watched raccoons and opossums, western tiger swallowtails and mourning cloak butterflies, and a host of arachnids that ply the bark, hunting for meals and building nests.

I am rather pleased to have Douglas-firs in our yard because they have long been one of my favorite plants, not simply because of their beauty but because of how they stimulated my interest in the stories that names tell. Consider the tree's common name, which was the first plant name that prompted me to trace its origin. Initially applied to the plants in 1833, in the *Penny Cyclopaedia* (produced by the optimistically named Society for the Diffusion of Useful Knowledge), the name honors Scottish botanist David Douglas, who had collected specimens along the Columbia River in 1825. He described them as "one of the most striking and graceful objects in Nature." The genus name *Pseudotsuga* is a lovely combination of Greek (*pseudo*, meaning "false") and Japanese (*tsuga*, meaning "hemlock"). The specific epithet also honors Archibald Menzies, the naturalist on George Vancouver's expedition to the Pacific Northwest in 1792.

Menzies brought the first specimens to Europe. While in Puget Sound, he wrote of being "regaled with a salubrious and vivifying air impregnated with the balsamic fragrance of the surrounding Pinery."

And, of course, long, long before Europeans arrived, the Indigenous peoples of the region had names for the tree, which still persist in more than three dozen languages. In Puget Sound, the Lushootseed name is čəbidac, which I have seen translated as "large-tree" or as a reference to the bark.

More than simply satisfying my intellectual curiosities, our Doug-firs and the ones in our neighbor's yard have also met the requirements of good habitat for a fascinating pair of species. For several winters, Bald Eagles have roosted in the Douglas-firs. They arrive around sundown, spend the night, and head out early in the morning. We often see them, but even when we don't, they make their presence clear by calling in that one-of-a-kind, squeaky-wheel sound they make. It is quite a pleasure to have a Bald Eagle as your alarm clock.

We also have been lucky enough to have visitations from Cooper's Hawks who nested a couple of houses away from us and regularly landed in our trees. One day after work, my wife and I were sitting in the backyard when two Cooper's Hawks flew through the yard and landed about twenty feet from us in one of our Douglas-firs. The birds sat for a bit, looked toward us, ignored us, and then took off. Their presence immediately took the edge off what had been a long day. Another time, I watched the female eat a rat, her mate observing close by. I later found the rodent's skull at the base of the tree. I have also found feathers from birds such as Spotted Towhees, as well as retched-up pellets brimming with feathers, fur, and bones. Nature and her tooth and claw in our little backyard.

Several years ago, one of our neighborhood Cooper's Hawks was banded. Two weeks later, he showed up in another backyard on Beacon Hill in south

Seattle, and the next day, across Lake Washington in Medina. Another Cooper's Hawk, banded in Volunteer Park, ended up in Oakland, California, three months later. What I might call my Cooper's Hawks, or you might call yours, are much more than that. We are merely lucky enough to lay a small and rather tenuous claim on birds that travel far and depend on good habitat in numerous locations.

For more than twenty-five years, my wife and I have never regretted living in our house, in large part because of the backyard. It has been a place of rest and rejuvenation, and during the years of Covid in particular, a critical sanctuary for us as we regularly sat out there sharing our thoughts at the end of our workdays. We have continued to enjoy our wilder visitors, from Barred Owls to a family of raccoons and even the yellow jackets who built an underground nest. As Dorothy said, "There's no place like home. There's no place like home," especially with a fine backyard.

Perchers, Pokers, and Pests

I like to think I pay attention, but the other day I realized that I have been missing a unique ecosystem every time I go for an urban walk. Wherever I go, I pass by utility poles. Holding up the wires that feed our modern lifestyles, these poles may be one of the most common and overlooked pieces of urban furniture.

What we now call utility poles began life as telegraph poles, when Samuel Morse and his colleagues erected them in 1844 to transmit telegraphs between Baltimore and Washington, DC. The wood poles soon snaked across the continent, and by the early twentieth century, they had become known as telephone, power, and utility poles. Modern estimates place the number of utility poles in the US at 150 million.

The first telephone appeared in Seattle on April 8, 1878, using the wires of the Puget Sound Telegraph Company, and by the 1890s, telephone poles lined downtown streets, often towering above the surrounding buildings. We now have 91,000 poles in the city. The tallest wood one is 95 feet. The oldest were put up in 1905 and are made of western redcedar, like 73 percent of all Seattle poles; 21 percent are Douglas-fir, and the rest unknown.

What attracted me to utility poles was a notice from Seattle City Light that they were going to replace a pole on our street. The city has long inspected and replaced poles but began an accelerated replacement program following an April 2019 storm that toppled twenty-six poles in Tukwila and sent two people to the hospital. A crew member replacing our pole told me that a Northern Flicker had damaged and weakened the pole. I wasn't surprised, as I had regularly seen and heard flickers banging their heads against the pole. (In Alabama, utility companies spend $3 million annually to replace woodpecker-damaged poles.)

In Seattle, squirrels, lichen, and birds are major exploiters of this habitat. For the squirrels, the poles are off- and on-ramps to an extensive high-wire highway that allows them to move quickly and usually skillfully, though I have seen squirrels struggle to negotiate their tightrope travel. Unfortunately, some squirrels get shocked to death on the wires, which can lead to power loss. According to the semiserious CyberSquirrel website, squirrels caused 1,252 outages worldwide from 1989 to 2019.

There is also the telephone pole beetle (*Micromalthus debilis*), named because an early specimen was found emerging from a chestnut telegraph pole. (They have been found in Vancouver, British Columbia, but not in Seattle.) These bugs are quite amazing; they can give birth parthenogenically— when an embryo develops from an unfertilized egg— and have remained unchanged, more or less, for at least twenty million years, though it's unclear how they lived before telephone poles came along.

As is often the case, lichen have adapted to a human-created substrate. Examples include *Lecanora conizaeoides*, which began to spread widely in cities as a result of the Industrial Revolution; *Hypogymnia physodes*, which has been used for air pollution studies; and *Evernia prunastri*, which was "ground up with rose petals to make a hair powder which whitened wigs,"

according to Frank Dobson in *Lichens: An Illustrated Guide to the British and Irish Species*. Always glad to be able to purvey thoughtful advice for when one needs to whiten one's wig!

Birds are probably the best-known pole users. Poles function as snags, providing perches (as do wires), nesting locations, and space for drumming and food caching. When I asked members of the local birding network, Tweeters, I was told of forty-eight pole-using species ranging in size from chickadee to Bald Eagle and alphabetically from Acorn Woodpecker to White-breasted Nuthatch.

Unfortunately, birds plus electricity do not add up to happy birds. They are regularly killed by electrocution and shock, especially larger birds, which more readily bridge the gap around energized conductors. One study estimated 504 Golden Eagles die this way annually. Birds also collide with wires, notably raptors with small home ranges and ones where the wires are between the birds' nests and their foraging locations. I am still always impressed to see a bird land on a wire; it's a supreme act of agility.

Conscientious maintenance to address electrocution and other animal-related utility pole interactions includes exclusion netting; chemical repellants or oil extracts of cumin, rosemary, and thyme; better insulation; an increased distance between wires and potential perches; perch guards; and hazing. Another solution, which one sees in Seattle and many other areas, is to build a platform just for the birds and devoid of wires. Seattle City Light has built several in the city, which Ospreys have colonized.

Unfortunately, poles have long created additional problems because of how they are treated for protection against rot and other issues of degradation. Throughout Puget Sound are numerous old mills and other sites where companies applied creosote, which has resulted in shoreline areas teeming with toxins such as polycyclic aromatic hydrocarbons (PAHs), PCBs, aromatic carrier oils, and dioxins and furans. (This process is not the lone source of PAHs in the Sound. They also come from combustion from vehicles and woodstoves.) Cleanup of these poisons is an ongoing process and often just as overlooked as the poles themselves.

A Potentially
Attractive Amenity

In his provocative book *The World Without Us*, Alan Weisman imagines what would happen to the planet if humans were to disappear. Fortunately, this has yet to happen—despite some of the really dumb things we do—but there is a city block in downtown Seattle where you used to be able to see what happens in our city without us.

The block sits between Third and Fourth Avenues and Cherry and James Streets. Long the site of the City's Public Safety Building, it became prime real estate for a wilder existence when the building was razed in 2005. Although designed by one of Seattle's legendary architecture firms, NBBJ, the building was later described as "this rather bland expression of governmental bureaucracy."

After liberating downtown of this exemplar of bland, the city sold the lot to Triad Development, which planned a forty-three-story building and another large public plaza. By 2015, Triad had yet to build, a victim of bad timing and pesky banks. Two years later, Triad sold the property to Bosa Development, which has proposed a fifty-seven-story tower and yet another plaza.

What was amazing and wonderful about this unbuilt-upon block, though, was that it was taken over by vegetation: blackberries, butterfly bushes, European weeping birches, and our native cottonwood, to name those I saw on one visit. The tallest tree was a fifty- to sixty-foot-tall cottonwood with shiny, heart-shaped leaves; other trees nearby were between twenty and thirty feet tall. Their small, lightweight seeds would have been wind travelers, riding the complicated currents that eddy and surge around the surrounding towers.

I did not see animals visiting this location on the several times I passed by this spot but suspect that birds and rodents took advantage of the food and habitat to establish a home base. Some were probably also availing themselves of a lack of predators, such as raccoons and coyotes, in their midst. Of course, the high walls wouldn't stop Peregrines, Merlins, and other avian predators from feasting.

Although most of the species I saw were non-native, and in fact are considered to be invasive (and superbly adapted to infiltrate spaces such as this), I still found reason to rejoice in this little spot of wildness in the heart of the city's urban core. Arguably the best thing we could have done for this location would have been simply not to build a massive tower and plaza (which would feature non-native plants anyway) and instead let nature take her course. Keep the block enclosed and think of the space as an experiment in entropy. If so many plants—in particular, the native cottonwood—were able to thrive in just seventeen years, imagine what we could see if we continue to leave it alone. As of spring 2024, the lot had been cleared, but apparently the builder ran out of money or energy, and vegetation has begun to return again.

I don't expect my vision for the future of this block to come to fruition, but I do think it would be good to allow more places in urban landscapes to have less management. We already do this for what we call empty lots, which tend not to be empty but have become home for many plants and animals. Some of my favorite green spaces in Seattle, such as Carkeek Park and certain sections along Thornton Creek, are areas where plants and animals are allowed to live and die naturally; no one comes in to clean up a broken-off limb, a fallen-over tree, or a decaying animal corpse. I understand that we cannot do this in most locations, but a city with more spaces devoted to the natural cycle of life and death is one that is better for all of its residents, human, plant, and animal.

Apple of My Eye

Handcycling along the Centennial Trail north of Arlington, my pal Scott and I like to track the flowering and fruiting progress of the half dozen or so apple trees growing there. The trail, like several in the region, began life as a train route that eventually gave way to the rails-to-trails movement. Our speculation is that the trees are wild ones that came from apples someone ate and tossed off the train. The seeds germinated and a tree was born. Of course, the proverbial bear (or other such beast) could have pooped the seeds out too.

I have found the same phenomenon along the Burke-Gilman Trail, originally the Seattle, Lake Shore and Eastern Railroad. One of the bigger apple trees grows just under the I-5 bridge over Lake Union. Like the Centennial Trail trees, the apple trees along the Burke-Gilman seem more connected to random human action than to a specific plan to populate the old train routes with fruit trees, although I do like that idea.

Like many cities, Seattle has had a long tradition of orchards and fruit trees. In 1860, Seattle had a settler population of a little over 300 people and nearly 3,000 apple trees, along with 197 pear and 177 cherry trees. Beyond the abundance of fruit, what astounds me is the different types of available fruit. For example, in 1878, a fruit-focused Seattleite could purchase 50 apple varieties, 40 pear, and 11 peach from one local nursery. All were "sure to ripen in this climate," according to the nursery's advertisement. Even in the best-stocked supermarkets in town, modern residents cannot hope to match these numbers.

Most of those trees would have been in what is now downtown Seattle and must have provided an amazing bounty for urban dwellers. The spring air would have been redolent with the enticing aroma of the trees' flowers, as well as filled with the wingbeats of pollinators. When the fruit matured, I like to imagine that neighborhood kids scoured their territories collecting fruit, most of which got eaten but some of which must have ended up missiling through the air as fruity weapons.

A few orchards still dot the urban landscape. Probably the best known and most diverse is along Pipers Creek in Carkeek Park. Planted at the end of the nineteenth century, the orchard contains numerous varieties of apple, as well as other fruits and nuts. There are still many, many small orchards or single trees dotting Seattle yards, which could have been part of larger orchards or the product of a fruitphilic homeowner.

Sadly, one of my favorite urban fruit trees no longer exists. Located in the Pike Place Market on Stewart Street between Western and First Avenues, the

cherry tree was removed sometime around 2013. The lone tree was one of several downtown cherries that artist Buster Simpson tried to protect in the 1970s and 1980s. Simpson believes, and I think he is correct, that the trees sprouted from seeds originally dropped or spit out by someone who had acquired the cherries at the market, ate some, and disposed of them.

I love the idea that feral fruit trees existed in downtown Seattle so recently and that many previously cultivated and wild fruit trees can still be found for those willing to search. Each of them tells a story, be it the connection between a resident and their home or simply the randomness of the natural world. As they say, one person's garbage is another's fruit tree.

Epilogue:
Hope Is a Baby Orca

In the summer of 2018, I grieved, with millions of people around the world. Our collective sadness focused on a twenty-year-old mother, Tahlequah, one of a dwindling number of orca who regularly visit Puget Sound. On July 24, Tahlequah had given birth to her second child, a daughter, who died within thirty minutes. For the next seventeen days, she carried the six-foot-long body of her dead offspring on a journey of more than a thousand miles. Finally, Tahlequah let her calf go. Our hearts broke.

Then, two years later, in September 2020, whale researchers announced Tahlequah had given birth again. The healthy and precocious boy calf, dubbed J57, was born in the Strait of Juan de Fuca, after an eighteen-month gestation. To paraphrase Emily Dickinson, hope is a baby orca in Puget Sound.

I am by nature an optimistic person, but I also became hopeful while working on my book *Homewaters*, from which this essay is adapted. Hope came in my discussions with biologists whose work to better understand animal life histories is helping to improve management of the Sound's inhabitants. For example, biologists used to think that rockfish, of which twenty-seven species occur in Puget Sound, had short life spans, akin to salmon, but now we know that rockfish live for more than a century. This has led to fundamental management changes, such as improved habitat protection and a fishing ban, which are giving the fish the decades that biologists now know are necessary to rebuild rockfish populations.

I find further hope in knowing that this place runs in the veins of the animals. By this, I mean that the Sound's plants and animals have evolved unique adaptations specific to the region's geology and ecology. The most famous are our salmon, who are well known for returning from the ocean to their natal streams. In the 2010s, they illustrated their homebody DNA by returning to the Elwha River after two dams that had blocked the river for a century were removed. As one biologist told me, the salmon "were able to return now because they have been doing this for thousands of years." What we have to do is give our wild residents the opportunity to realize their potential.

One way that we have begun to create this opportunity plays out in our changing relationship to the natural world. For most of the post-settlement history of Puget Sound, residents viewed the region as a place to exploit oysters, coal, salmon, and trees. But in the past few decades, people have become more focused on sustainability, respect for other species, and stewardship. They recognize the fragility, beauty, and resilience of the Sound and have been working toward what author and conservationist Wallace Stegner called a "society to match the scenery."

I also see this changing relationship with Native people; after more than a century of being disenfranchised and disrespected, they have now become important players in ecological and political decisions. It was inspiring to see how Tribal groups helped stop the largest coal port ever proposed in North America and worked to ensure a court decision calling for the removal of hundreds of culverts that restricted access to salmon habitat.

Because of societal, scientific, and governmental changes, Puget Sound is in better shape now than it has been in its recent past. We have enacted new laws and regulations that have led to a cleaner and healthier ecosystem, and we are no longer harvesting fish at unsustainable rates or allowing factories to pollute as they once did. Instead, we are looking at ways to preserve and restore habitat. The activists and scientists I spoke to are not naive enough to think that we can restore Puget Sound to what it was before the arrival of Europeans, but they say that they are inspired by the abundance of the past, the potential for further recovery, and the resilience of species such as salmon and rockfish.

The hope that I gained through my increased understanding of the human and natural history of Puget Sound is not of the wishy-washy "I hope I win the lottery" sort. My hope goes hand in hand with hard work. It may require that each of us needs to change, that we recognize and acknowledge that we have a role to play, and that we understand we are part of the problem, as well as part of the solution.

I have also begun to reconsider the phrase "Nothing I do makes a difference." I have long been daunted by it, thinking that no matter what I do, it has little impact relative to the big polluters and consumers. I have found by simply turning that phrase around and saying, "Everything I do makes a difference," I feel more empowered.

As a member of my community, I am deeply connected to what's around me. I can make it better. I won't always do what's right, but I can work toward that goal of a better place. I know that it won't be easy. It will take money and commitment and courage and knowledge. But I also know that I can draw inspiration from the adaptations of the more-than-human species that live here, as well as from the humans who are doing good work. For all of that, I am hopeful.

Acknowledgments

Writing a book is always a privilege and pleasure for me, in large part because of the many people with whom I interact in the process. All of the following people have played a part in this book, and I am honored to thank them.

As always, the support and encouragement of the Unspeakables has been priceless.

Over the past years, I have had a weekly virtual date with my college friends Jeff Moline and Scott Wanek. Your decades of friendship have helped my writing in uncountable ways, mostly good.

I have been blessed by two mentors, Carol Doig and Tony Angell, whose unwavering and generous support and enthusiasm means more to me than they realize.

As anyone who has spent time with me knows, I like to ask questions. I appreciate the following who answered those questions and gave me suggestions for stories: Bud Anderson, Becky Andrews, Brian Atwater, Feliks Banel, Knute Berger, Butch Bernhardt, Nick Bond, Derek Booth, Fred Brown, Ray Buckley, David Buerge, Valarie Bunn, Barb Burrill, Bobbie Buzzell, Tish Cameron, Trevor Contreras, Dave Cook, Darrel Cowan, Sarah Croston, David Dethier, Richard Droker, James Dwyer, Clay Eals, Stephanie Earls, Taha Ebrahimi, Ron Edge, Anna Elam, Maureen Elenga,

Andres Elgorriaga, LisaRuth Elliott, Violet Snu'Meethia Elliott, Annie Ferguson, Sarah Gage, Carrie Garrison-Laney, Joe Gaydos, David Giblin, Jason Groves, Jessie Hale, Liz Hammond-Kaarremaa, Martin Haulena, Yasmine Hentati, Thomas Hörnschemeyer, Jeff Jensen, Glen Kalisz, Dan Kerlee, Rob Ketcherside, Bob Kopperl, Bill Laprade, Ray Larson, Audrey Lin, Mike Lindblom, Robert Long, Michael MacDonald, Jaime Martin, Shauna McDaniel, Ian Miller, Richard Miller, Josh Morris, Martin Muller, George Mustoe, Liz Nesbitt, Jeffrey Karl Ochsner, Jen Ott, Boyd Pratt, Pat Pringle, David Rash, Whitney Rearick, Tom Reese, Brandy Rinck, Nelson Salisbury, Jean Sherrad, Brian Sherrod, Hugh Shipman, Buster Simpson, Garry Smith, Evan Sugden, Kathy Troost, Dave Tucker, Nancy Turner, Louis Uccellini, Austin Watson, Candace Wellman, Katie Whitlock, Stuart Williams, Marie Wong, and Bill Woodward.

What began as sort of a whim has grown into this book, in part because of those who subscribe to my *Street Smart Naturalist* newsletter. Knowing that you are out there keeps me motivated and continues to make the newsletters enjoyable for me to write. Your generosity has been, and continues to be, inspiring and important in allowing me to devote my time to creating these essays for the newsletter.

I feel lucky to be back again with the gang at Mountaineers Books, including Emily White, who championed this book from the beginning; Jenn Kepler and her splendid copyediting; and Janet Kimball, who has made sure the book leapt through the hurdles of editing and production. And, of course, a big thank-you to Kate Rogers, whose ongoing support drew me back into her community.

Normally, I have to go through all the work of finding artwork. It has been wonderful to be paired with Elizabeth Person, whose stunning images brought life to the book, and the book to life.

I have said it before and will continue to say it forever. Marjorie Kittle, you rock my world, and as always, you were essential to the creation of these essays in far too many ways to list.

LAND ACKNOWLEDGMENT

I live and work on the land of the Coast Salish peoples and am trying to honor with gratitude the land and those who have inhabited it since time immemorial. I know that I have much more to learn and hope to continue that journey.

Selected References

YOUNG AND RESTLESS

Campbell, Sarah K. "Duwamish No. 1 Site: A Lower Puget Sound Shell Midden." Office of Public Archaeology Research Report 1. Seattle: University of Washington, 1981.

Ludwin, R. S., Robert Dennis, Deborah Carver, et al. "Dating the 1700 Cascadia Earthquake: Great Coastal Earthquake in Native Stories." *Seismological Research Letters* 76, no. 2 (March/April 2005): 140–148.

Ludwin, R. S., C. P. Thrush, K. James, et al. "Serpent Spirit-Power Stories Along the Seattle Fault." *Seismological Research Letters* 76, no. 4 (July/August 2005): 426–431.

DEAD TREES TELL NO LIES

Black, Bryan A., Jessie K. Pearl, Charlotte L. Pearson, et al. "A Multifault Earthquake Threat for Seattle Metropolitan Region Revealed by Mass Tree Mortality." *Science Advances* 9, no. 39 (September 2023).

WELL-TRAVELED CEMENT

Pratt, Boyd C. *Lime: Quarrying and Limemaking in the San Juan Islands.* Friday Harbor, WA: Mulno Cove, 2022.

SLIP SLIDING AWAY

Evans, Stephen. "Draining Seattle—WPA Landslide Stabilization Projects, 1935–1941." *Washington Geology* 22, no. 4 (December 1994): 3–10.

OTTERS IN OUR MIDST

Wainstein, Michelle, Louisa B. Harding, Sandra M. O'Neill, et al. "Highly Contaminated River Otters (*Lutra canadensis*) Are Effective Biomonitors of Environmental Pollutant Exposure." *Environmental Monitoring and Assessment* 194, no. 10 (2022).

CLAM SLAMMING

Barash, David P., Patrick Donovan, and Rinda Myrick. "Clam Dropping Behavior of the Glaucous-Winged Gull (*Larus glaucescens*)." *Wilson Bulletin* 87, no. 1 (March 1975): 60–64.

Cristol, Daniel L., Jennifer G. Akst, Michael K. Curatola, et al. "Age-Related Differences in Foraging Ability among Clam-Dropping Herring Gulls (*Larus argentatus*)." *Wilson Journal of Ornithology* 129, no. 2 (2017): 301–310.

A SINGULAR SLUG

Walker, Bryant. "Foreign Land Snails in Michigan." *Occasional Papers of the Museum of Zoology*, no. 58 (1918): 1–3.

TAILS OF THE CITY: CATTAIL

Ostapkowicz, Joanna, Dana Lepofsky, Rick Shulting, and Albert (Sonny) McHalsie. "The Use of Cattail (*Typha latifolia* L.) Down as a Sacred Substance by the Interior and Coast Salish of British Columbia." *Journal of Ethnobiology* 21, no. 2 (Winter 2001): 77–90.

TAILS OF THE CITY: HORSETAIL

Brooks, R. R., J. Holzbecher, and D. E. Ryan. "Horsetails (Equisetum) as Indirect Indicators of Gold Mineralization." *Journal of Geochemical Exploration* 16 (1981): 21–26.

THE DEVILS' CLUB

Turner, Nancy. "Traditional Uses of Devil's Club By Native Peoples in Western North America." *Journal of Ethnobiology* 2, no. 1 (1982): 17–38.

Harrer, Laurie E. F., and Taal Levi. "The Primacy of Bears as Seed Dispersers in Salmon-Bearing Ecosystems." *Ecosphere* 9, no. 1 (January 2018): 1–15.

PERCHERS, POKERS, AND PESTS

Slater, Steven J. "Conservation Letter: Raptors and Overhead Electrical Systems." *Journal of Raptor Research* 54, no. 2 (2020): 198–203.

A POTENTIALLY ATTRACTIVE AMENITY

Woodbridge, Sally B., and Roger Montgomery. *A Guide to Architecture in Washington State*. Seattle: University of Washington Press, 1980.

Further Reading

Buerge, David M. *Chief Seattle and the Town That Took His Name*. Seattle: Sasquatch Books, 2017.

Cummings, BJ. *The River That Made Seattle: A Human and Natural History of the Duwamish*. Seattle: University of Washington Press, 2020.

Ebrahimi, Taha. *Street Trees of Seattle: An Illustrated Walking Guide*. Seattle: Sasquatch Books, 2024.

Gunter, Erna. *Ethnobotany of Western Washington*, rev. ed. Seattle: University of Washington Press, 1973.

Harmon, Alexandra. *Indians in the Making: Ethnic Relations and Indian Identities around Puget Sound*. Berkeley: University of California Press, 1998.

Haupt, Lyanda Lynn. *Rare Encounters with Ordinary Birds*. Seattle: Sasquatch Books, 2002.

Morgan, Murray. *Skid Road: An Informal Portrait of Seattle*. Seattle: University of Washington Press, 2018.

Thrush, Coll. *Native Seattle: Histories from the Crossing-Over Place*. Seattle: University of Washington Press, 2007.

Turner, Nancy. *Food Plants of British Columbia Indians: Coastal Peoples*. Victoria: British Columbia Provincial Museum, 1975.

Williams, David B. *Too High and Too Steep: Reshaping Seattle's Topography*. Seattle: University of Washington Press, 2015.

About the Author

David B. Williams is an author, naturalist, and tour guide whose award-winning book *Homewaters: A Human and Natural History of Puget Sound* is a deep exploration of the stories of this beautiful waterway. He is also the author of the award-winning book *Too High and Too Steep: Reshaping Seattle's Topography*, as well as *Seattle Walks: Discovering History and Nature in the City, Spirit Whales and Sloth Tales: Fossils of Washington State* (co-authored with Elizabeth Nesbitt), and *Cairns: Messengers in Stone*. Williams's website is geologywriter.com, where you can learn more about his books and subscribe to his free weekly newsletter, the *Street Smart Naturalist*.

MOUNTAINEERS BOOKS, including its two imprints, Skipstone and Braided River, is a leading publisher of quality outdoor recreation, sustainability, and conservation titles. As a 501(c)(3) nonprofit, we are committed to supporting the environmental and educational goals of our organization by providing expert information on human-powered adventure, sustainable practices at home and on the trail, and preservation of wilderness.

Our publications are made possible through the generosity of donors, and through sales of 700 titles on outdoor recreation, sustainable lifestyle, and conservation. To donate, purchase books, or learn more, visit us online:

MOUNTAINEERS BOOKS

1001 SW Klickitat Way, Suite 201 • Seattle, WA 98134
800-553-4453 • mbooks@mountaineersbooks.org
www.mountaineersbooks.org

An independent nonprofit publisher since 1960

YOU MAY ALSO LIKE: